SOCIAL PHILOSOPHY

PRENTICE-HALL FOUNDATIONS OF PHILOSOPHY SERIES

Virgil Aldrich	Philosophy of Art
William Alston	Philosophy of Language
Stephen Barker	Philosophy of Mathematics
Roderick Chisholm	Theory of Knowledge
William Dray	Philosophy of History
Joel Feinberg	Social Philosophy
William Frankena	Ethics
Carl Hempel	Philosophy of Natural Science
John Hick	Philosophy of Religion
David Hull	Philosophy of Biological Science
Willard Van Orman Quine	Philosophy of Logic
Richard Rudner	Philosophy of Social Science
Wesley Salmon	Logic
Jerome Shaffer	Philosophy of Mind
Richard Taylor	Metaphysics

Elizabeth and Monroe Beardsley, editors

SOCIAL PHILOSOPHY

Joel Feinberg
THE ROCKEFELLER UNIVERSITY

PRENTICE HALL
Englewood Cliffs, New Jersey 07632

Library of Congress Cataloging in Publication Data

Feinberg, Joel
  Social philosophy.

  (Foundations of philosophy series)
  Bibliography: p.
  1. Political science. I. Title.
JA71.45   320'.01   72-5433
ISBN 0-13-817262-5
ISBN 0-13-817254-4 (pbk.)

©1973 by Prentice-Hall, Inc.
A Division of Simon & Schuster
Englewood Cliffs, New Jersey 07632

Printed in the United States of America

30 29 28 27 26 25 24 23 22

ISBN   0-13-817254-4

Prentice-Hall International (UK) Limited, *London*
Prentice-Hall of Australia Pty. Limited, *Sydney*
Prentice-Hall Canada Inc., *Toronto*
Prentice-Hall Hispanoamericana, S.A., *Mexico*
Prentice-Hall of India Private Limited, *New Delhi*
Prentice-Hall of Japan, Inc., *Tokyo*
Simon & Schuster Asia Pte. Ltd., *Singapore*
Editora Prentice-Hall do Brasil, Ltda., *Rio de Janeiro*

To the memory of my father,

Abraham J. Feinberg (1888–1956)

FOUNDATIONS OF PHILOSOPHY

Many of the problems of philosophy are of such broad relevance to human concerns, and so complex in their ramifications, that they are, in one form or another, perennially present. Though in the course of time they yield in part to philosophical inquiry, they may need to be rethought by each age in the light of its broader scientific knowledge and deepened ethical and religious experience. Better solutions are found by more refined and rigorous methods. Thus, one who approaches the study of philosophy in the hope of understanding the best of what it affords will look for both fundamental issues and contemporary achievements.

Written by a group of distinguished philosophers, the Foundations of Philosophy Series aims to exhibit some of the main problems in the various fields of philosophy as they stand at the present stage of philosophical history.

While certain fields are likely to be represented in most introductory courses in philosophy, college classes differ widely in emphasis, in method of instruction, and in rate of progress. Every instructor needs freedom to change his course as his own philosophical interests, the size and makeup of his classes, and the needs of his students vary from year to year. The nineteen volumes in the Foundations of Philosophy Series—each complete in itself, but complementing the others—offer a new flexibility to the instructor, who can create his own textbook by combining several volumes as he wishes, and can choose different combinations at different times. Those volumes that are not used in an introductory course will be found valuable, along with other texts or collections of readings, for the more specialized upper-level courses.

Elizabeth Beardsley / *Monroe Beardsley*

ACKNOWLEDGMENTS

A large part of Chapter 1 of this book appears in expanded form in "The Idea of a Free Man," in *Educational Judgments: Papers in the Philosophy of Education,* ed. James Doyle (London: Routledge & Kegan Paul, 1973). Parts of Chapters 2 and 3 are contained in my essay " 'Harmless Immoralities' and Offensive Nuisances," in *Issues in Law and Morality,* ed. Norman Care and Thomas Trelogan (Cleveland: The Press of Case Western Reserve University, 1973). Another part of Chapter 3 is contained in my "Legal Paternalism," *Canadian Journal of Philosophy,* Vol. 1 (1971). Various parts of Chapter 4 are contained in my paper "The Nature and Value of Rights," *The Journal of Value Inquiry,* Vol. 4 (1970). I am grateful to the publishers of the essays mentioned above and to Prentice-Hall, Inc. for their generous consent to these duplications.

Joël Feinberg

CONTENTS

SOCIAL PHILOSOPHY

Introduction

The scope of social philosophy is less precisely defined than that of most other conventional "branches" of philosophy. Conceived very broadly, social philosophy includes problems treated in other volumes of the Foundations of Philosophy series. Questions about the methodology of the social sciences are dealt with in Richard Rudner's *Philosophy of Social Science;* theories about the foundation of ethical judgment are criticized in William Frankena's *Ethics;* and distinctively political questions (for example, those concerning social institutions of a peculiarly political kind, such as "the state," and such concepts and norms as "legitimacy," "authority," "consent," and the obligation of obedience) are treated at length in Gerald MacCallum's *Political Philosophy.* Even when problems of these kinds are assigned to other areas of philosophy, we are left with a large, miscellaneous set of philosophical questions about social relations. I can treat here only a small subset of that remainder, those issues that seem to be of especially vital contemporary concern, and which are also highly representative of the problems of social philosophy in its narrower conception.

Such problems are of two basic kinds. There are *conceptual problems* requiring analysis and clarification of the central concepts used in social theory and in everyday discourse about social questions, and there are general *normative questions* calling for the formulation of principles to guide decision and judgment making in the controversial realm of social policy. The answers to the conceptual questions are generally (with only a few exceptions and qualifications) neutral in respect to the major social controversies. To handle them adequately we must reflect on what we normally mean when we employ certain words, and what we had better mean if we are to communicate efficiently, avoid paradox, and achieve general coherence. The normative questions, on the other hand, require us to discard our neutrality and to plunge into the moral arena where the interests and ideals of men are fully engaged, and conflicting practical norms and policies contend for our allegiance.

The social concepts to be examined in this book are themselves of two kinds: first, those that express *social ideals,* especially the ideals of liberty, justice, and equality, and second, various key concepts used in statements of normative principles, e.g., "harm," "benefit," "want," "need," "claim," and "right." For example, we can ask just how we are to understand the concept of liberty itself, how it can be made as coherent and precise as possible without begging any substantive questions about how liberty is best distributed. Then, when we come to the most important normative questions about liberty, such as those asking the conditions under which liberty is properly restricted, we shall have to consider critically various alternative answers. That task will presuppose that we have a clear conception of the central terms ("harm," "benefit," and so on) in which the various liberty-limiting principles are formulated. The relevance of the latter conceptual questions is easily appreciated when they arise naturally in the course of normative philosophizing, where they must be answered as a means to the end of choosing practical principles; however, persons of a reflective disposition may also make the pursuit of answers to the conceptual questions an end in itself.

The primary normative questions investigated in this book are those whose answers take the form of "liberty-limiting principles," lists of human rights, and material principles of economic justice. It is convenient to think of these problems as questions for some hypothetical and abstract political body. An answer to the question of when liberty should be limited or how wealth ideally should be distributed, for example, could be used to guide not only moralists, but also legislators and judges toward reasonable decisions in particular cases where interests, rules, or the liberties of different parties appear to conflict. In posing such questions about liberty and justice, the philosopher is asking what coercive laws and procedures would be created by an ideally reasonable legislature in a community whose history, customs, and political institutions resemble our own. We must think of an ideal legislator as somewhat abstracted from the full legislative context, in that he is free to appeal directly to the public interest unencumbered by the need to please voters, to make "deals" with colleagues, or any other merely "political" considerations. (Philosophical policy making at this abstract level may thus be somewhat less complex and difficult than actual legislative problems.) The principles of the ideal legislator (or constitution drafter) may not be totally decisive in the deliberations of the actual rational legislator, but they are still of the first practical importance, since they provide a target for our aspirations and a standard for judging our successes and failures.

Correct general principles and ultimate policies do not reveal themselves spontaneously, nor are they deduced from self-evident principles. The only way to arrive at them is to begin with those singular judgments and attitudes about particular social issues in which we have the greatest confidence, and attempt to extract their implicit rationales. We then tentatively apply the extracted principles to perplexing borderline cases, revising the general principle where necessary to accommodate the specific judgment, and modifying the particular attitude where required by a well-tested or deeply entrenched general principle, always aiming at the ideal of a comprehensive personal and interpersonal coherence in which singular judgments and general principles stand in a "reflective equilibrium." John Leonard's advice about education in social policy making applies equally well to social philosophy, the most general social policy making:

Demonstrate how complicated policy-making really is. *That* would be an education. The teacher would pay his dues as a citizen; the student would learn that truth is not some instantaneous revelation, immutably obvious in the fires of an existential moment, but only the grubby approximation of a shared ideal.[1]

[1] John Leonard, "The Last Word: Policy I for Freshmen," *The New York Times Book Review*, September 26, 1971, p. 63.

CHAPTER ONE

The Concept
of Freedom

1. FREEDOM AND CONSTRAINT

There was a time when to call a man "free" was simply to describe his legal rights and duties and to contrast them with those of a slave.[1] In time the word "free" became the name not only of a legal status but also of a set of character virtues especially becoming to a man of free status. "Free" in this sense is opposed to "servile," which was used to refer to qualities characteristic of slaves and hence inappropriate in a freeman. A servile person is "alternately fawning and insolent";[2] a free man, having nothing to fear, is dignified and deliberate, and can look any man in the eye. In asking what freedom truly is, we may be asking for a fuller account of these qualities; in describing a given man as free, we may be simply ascribing such virtues to him. It is more likely, however, that our contemporary interest in a person's freedom is not simply a concern over his legal status or his character. What then are we saying of a man when we say that he is free?

[1] See C. S. Lewis, *Studies in Words* (Cambridge: Cambridge University Press, 1961), pp. 111 ff.
[2] Lewis, *Studies in Words*, p. 14.

4

We may be saying very little, for the word "free," without further specification, is often incompletely informative. Most general ascriptions of freedom are best understood as *elliptical,* or abbreviative for some longer expression. There are three kinds of ellipses that can render sentences about freedom obscure; depending on the context, a given ascription of freedom may contain each or any of them. To make such sentences more informative, we may have to add specifications of what someone is free *from,* or is free *to* do, or more precisely *who* it is whose freedom is at issue.

If a stranger casually informs you that he is free, you may have little idea of what he intends to convey until he tells you what he is free *from.* "Has he just escaped from prison, from his debts, from his wife, from his sins?"[3] Until this further specification is forthcoming, you can infer only that he is asserting (with pleasure) the absence of *something* which he regards as an impediment or constraint.[4] Perhaps you can guess what his desires are, but you must know something of his special circumstances to know what barrier to those desires he claims to be missing.

Because of the intimate tie between constraints and desires, it is natural to think of the abridgment of freedom as necessarily productive of frustration. When we are constrained in the most obvious cases, our wants are denied their satisfaction. That condition is frustrating, and frustration is a kind of unhappiness, which of course is an evil. It may be for this reason that we are so certain that freedom, which is the absence of constraint and hence of frustration-unhappiness, is a Good Thing. But there is another tendency in our ordinary thought (or another conception of freedom) which denies the logical link between constraint and frustration. According to this conception, one can be constrained without being frustrated. A man can be having the time of his life while locked in a room, either because he doesn't know that the door is locked or because he doesn't care;[5] an armed guard with a gun at one's head can "force" one to vote for the candidate one had intended to vote for all along for one's own reasons. These examples of constraint and compulsion are certainly not examples of frustration. The constraints illustrated do not affect one's actual desires, although they do restrict one's opportunities and narrow one's alternatives. The freedom they destroy can be called a hypothetical or

---

[3] Maurice Cranston, *Freedom, A New Analysis* (London: Longmans, Green & Co. Ltd., 1953), p. 3.

[4] The distinction between a constraint and a *compulsion* is a matter of diction. When we are constrained, we are prevented from doing, i.e., forced to omit; when we are compelled, we are prevented from omitting, i.e., forced to do. In the case of constraint, we cannot do what we (might) want to do; in the case of compulsion, we must do what we (might) not want to do. Nevertheless, for convenience, I shall use the word "constraint" for both constraints and compulsions.

[5] Cf. John Locke, *An Essay Concerning Human Understanding* (New York: Dover Publications, Inc., 1959), Vol. II, p. 317.

dispositional liberty, since *if* (contrary to fact) one were to choose to leave the locked room or to vote for the other candidate, *then* one would be blocked and frustrated.

Why should anyone value freedom for desires he merely might come to have, or possibly could have in the future, when at any given time he can do what he wants without frustration? This question is no mere theoretical puzzle. We condemn and fight foreign tyrants for restricting the dispositional liberties of their subjects, even when we know that because of ignorance, resignation, or love of an inspirational leader, few subjects feel really deprived. Why complain that a subject is not free to criticize his Führer when he *loves* the Führer and agrees with all his policies? One answer that suggests itself immediately is that merely "possible" desires have a way of becoming actual. We can rarely foresee with certainty the course of changes either in ourselves or in our circumstances, and so we feel much safer if there are genuine alternatives available, even though we have no present use for them. Moreover, even if there is no chance that our desires will ever change, it is reassuring to know that there are always alternatives, just in case. The love of freedom can be a love of breathing space, of room to maneuver, of a chance to change one's mind.

A strong case has also been made for the superiority of freedom conceived simply as the absence of present frustration. The ancient Stoics and Epicureans argued that the quest for freedom viewed as "breathing space" is itself bound to be a source of frustration to the desires that impel it, whereas total freedom from frustration is within every man's power and can be found in totalitarian as well as "free" societies. To be perfectly free, they argued, is always to be able to do what you actually want, at the time, to do. To gain this freedom one must either be powerful enough to bend the whole world to one's will, or flexible enough to adapt one's will to what must inevitably happen. Surely the latter is the easier course. If you adjust your desires so that you always want to do what you must do, then you can never be disappointed. "Demand not that events happen as you wish," cautions Epictetus, "but wish them to happen as they do happen, and you will get on well."[6]

In the contrast between freedom conceived in the "actually occurrent" and "dispositional" ways, two different ideals of liberty are involved: minimizing frustration versus maximizing the number of genuine alternatives open to a person, whatever the effect on his states of mind. According to the first conception, a person is free only to the extent that he can do what he wants to do when he wants to do it; according to the second, a person is free only if he can do considerably more than what he wants to do. Deciding which kind of liberty is the more suitable *ideal* may involve conflicting standards of value, but reflection will show that, ques-

6 Epictetus, *The Enchiridion*, VIII.

tions of value aside, the dispositional analysis gives a more accurate account of our ordinary understanding of what liberty *is* (or what the word "free" *means*).

Suppose that John Doe can do one thousand things at time *t,* but not the one thing he wants most to do, whereas Richard Roe can only do one thing at time *t,* but it happens to be the thing he wants most to do. If freedom is understood as simple absence of frustration, then Roe is freer than Doe. However, on the dispositional or "breathing space" model, Doe is not only freer than Roe, but Roe is totally unfree, for if there is only one thing that circumstances permit him to do, then he is compelled (however willingly) to do that thing. That the dispositional analysis of freedom is closer to common sense is further shown by consideration of the case in which Doe can do one thousand things *including* what he most wants to do, whereas Roe can do only the thing he most wants to do. On the absence of frustration model, Doe and Roe do not differ at all in respect to freedom, even though Doe and Roe are equally content and Roe is forced to act with a bayonet in his back! These rough hypothetical examples strongly suggest that freedom is one thing, and want-satisfaction (or contentment) another.

Nevertheless, it may be true that (dispositional) freedom is *valuable* only as a means to want-satisfaction. If that is so, then there is no ground for preferring freedom if our want-satisfactions are guaranteed without it. But however we value freedom, whether as means, only or also as an end in itself, freedom should not be confused with the other goods to which it can be related. Some may reach the hasty conclusion that, whatever freedom is, it must be importantly good. They are then led to deny that freedom could ever conflict with other things that are importantly good, that a freedom that conflicts with contentment, for example, could not be a genuine freedom worthy of that glittering name. It is more honest and perceptive to admit that freedom is one value among many, and sometimes may not be worth its price as calculated in terms of other values. Sometimes the straightest road to happiness is through constraint, but that doesn't show that "true freedom" is constraint. It shows only that freedom is one thing and happiness another, and that one can't always have everything.

Not all forms of constraint and compulsion are of equal interest to the social and political philosopher. If there is a special kind of freedom that deserves to be called "political freedom" or "liberty," it must consist in the absence of that one special kind of constraint called *coercion,* which is the deliberate forceful interference in the affairs of human beings by other human beings. Coercion takes two main forms: direct forcing or preventing, such as by prodding with bayonets or imprisoning, and a threat of harm clearly backed up by enforcement power. In cases of coercion via threat, there is a sense in which the victim is left with a choice.

He can comply or he can suffer the (probable) consequences. But if the alternative to compliance is some unthinkable disaster—such as the death of a child—then there is really no choice but to comply. In intermediate cases, between the extremes of overwhelmingly coercive threats and mere attractive offers, the threat, in effect, puts a price tag on noncompliance and leaves it up to the threatened person to decide whether the price is worth paying. The higher the price of noncompliance, the less eligible it will seem for his choice. For this intermediate range, threats are like burdens on a man's back, rather than shackles, or bonds, or bayonets. They make one of his alternatives more difficult, but not impossible. This is the way in which taxes on socially undesirable conduct can be said to be coercive. Although they discourage without actually prohibiting, they can quite effectively prevent.

We have still to discuss the troublesome distinction between constraints (including forms of coercion) and mere *inabilities*. "It is not lack of freedom," said Helvetius, "not to fly like an eagle or swim like a whale."[7] But why not? If a human being wants desperately to do just those things, won't his desire be frustrated? He will be prevented from doing what he wants just as effectively by his own physical constitution and the laws of nature as others are by policemen's bayonets and the laws of the state.

The sensitive theorist will feel two contrary inclinations at this point. Having already embraced the view that freedom essentially involves absence of constraint to actual and possible desires, he may wish to preserve a symmetry between different sorts of constraints, and make his analysis as general as possible. Consequently, he may reason as follows. Wherever it is meaningful to speak of a possible desire, it must be equally meaningful to speak of a possible constraint. Anything, even a law of nature, can be a constraint to some kind of desire, and constraints can be internal as well as external. People are constantly prevented from doing what they want, or what they might come to want, by their own poverty, weakness, and ignorance. Whatever prevents satisfaction of an actual or hypothetical desire is a *constraint;* since freedom is the absence of constraint, it follows that we are unfree to do what we are unable to do, whatever the source of our inability.

On the other hand, it may be confusing the issue to let the words "free" and "unfree" do so much work. There may be no limit to what we *wish* as the object of idle fancies, but not everything wished can be seriously *desired*. A five year old might wish that he could walk on the sun, as an adult might wish that he were young again, but it is conceptually impossible for anyone who understands these fanciful objectives to *want* them to come into existence. We should think of freedom as related to actual and possible wants rather than idle wishes. Even if we concede (as we should not)

7 As quoted by Isaiah Berlin, *Two Concepts of Liberty* (Oxford: Clarendon Press, 1961), p. 7.

that there is no limit to what one can come to want or desire, the limits on what we can do or be are strict. I can lament that I was not born Winston Churchill, that I am not a mathematical genius or a potential weight-lifting champion, that I cannot give birth to a baby, or both be and not be at the same time. But to characterize these natural limitations as restrictions on my freedom would be to base a lament on a platitude. "To be," wrote Santayana, "is to be something in particular." That I am one thing rather than another is not so much a restriction on my freedom as a necessary consequence of my existing at all. Still, if I had been born into one of the lower classes in *Brave New World,* having been created in a test tube and deliberately conditioned to be inferior, I suppose my lament that I am not *free* to realize a higher potential might be at least intelligible. Although the line between inabilities that are also unfreedoms and those that are not is obviously hard to draw, we should make every effort to draw it with precision, for unless *some* incapacities are *not* considered to be unfreedoms, perfect freedom itself will be an utterly empty and unapproachable ideal.

In social and political discourse, at least, unfreedom usually means not just any kind of inability, but rather inability of one special kind—namely, that induced directly or indirectly by the coercive power of other human beings. Perhaps the wisest course is to follow Isaiah Berlin, who claims that "Mere incapacity to attain your goal is not lack of political freedom."[8] It is important, however, to point out that it is the presence of the word "political" in the quoted sentence that allows it to be incontrovertibly true. We can then compromise between our conflicting inclinations by saying that political and social philosophy are concerned with freedom only when conceived as the absence of coercion by others. Ethics and metaphysics may quite properly concern themselves with more varied sorts of constraints, and thus we can assume for a much wider range of cases that we are not free to do what we are unable to do—though, as we have seen, there must be a limit to this principle even in ethics and metaphysics.

A final caveat. Often poverty, illness, ignorance, and other "internal and negative constraints" are themselves the indirect results of deliberately imposed and modifiable social arrangements. In such cases, we have every right to refer to them as restrictions on political liberty.[9]

2. FREEDOM FROM...   When a speaker asserts that he is free, he might
AND FREEDOM TO...   know quite clearly what he is free *to* do, but be
                                       quite vague about what constraint he is free *from.*
Perhaps all he means to convey is that *nothing* now prevents him from doing *X,* in which case the intended emphasis of his remark is on the option now

8 Berlin, *Two Concepts of Liberty,* p. 7.
9 A point well made by Berlin, *Two Concepts of Liberty,* p. 8.

open to him, and no specific descriptions of missing constraints are necessary to fill out his meaning. As we have seen, if the X in question is something most of us are normally free to do anyway, we may be puzzled by the speaker's remark until he specifies more narrowly which former constraint to his desire to do X has now been removed. When this puzzlement does not arise, no description of specific missing constraints is required for clarity.

On other occasions, the primary or exclusive emphasis of a speaker's assertion of freedom may rest on a specific missing constraint. He may, for example, claim to "be free" simply because one hated barrier to a given desire has been lifted, even though other barriers to that same desire still remain. All of the emphasis of his remark is thus on the removed constraint, and his newly asserted freedom does not imply that he can yet *do* any more than he formerly could. He is free *from* one barrier to his doing X, and that may seem to be blessed relief from an oppressive burden, but he may still be unable to do X. In an extreme limiting case, a speaker may have no concern with future *actions* whatever, and the existence of new alternatives for choice may be no part of his intended meaning when he asserts that he is free *from C*. He may be exclusively preoccupied with the removal of some odious condition, quite apart from any effect that removal might have on his *other* desires or options. He may simply hate his chains and conceive his "freedom" to consist entirely in their removal. In this not uncommon case, freedom from... implies no new freedom to... other than the freedom of being without the specific thing one is said to be free from.

More typically, when we use the language of missing constraint, we imply that there is something we want to do (or might come to want to do) that the constraint prevents us from doing, and that to be free from that constraint is to be able to do it. In the typical case, then, "freedom from" and "freedom to" are two sides of the same coin, each involved with the other, and not two radically distinct kinds of freedom, as some writers have suggested. Indeed, it is difficult fully to characterize a given constraint without mentioning the desires it does or can constrain (that is, desires other than the exclusive desire to be relieved of *it*). The man outside of divorce court who tells us that he is now free (presumably *from* the woman who was his wife) has not communicated much until he specifies which desires he can now satisfy that he could not satisfy when he was married. Without this further specification, we know only that he is without a wife and quite happy about it; but then, as we have seen, that may be all that he had in mind when he said that he was free.

At any given time, a person is free to do some things but not free to do others, just as he may be free of one kind of constraint to a given desire but not free of another. To ask whether a person is "free" without any further specification, may demand a long and detailed answer. (Of

course, the context usually gives clues to the particular desires and constraints being inquired about.) The situation is even more obscure when
political partisans campaign for "freedom," or freedom as qualified by
some adjective. Maurice Cranston quite rightly advises us to "call for the
full version of all such abbreviated slogans."[10]

The full version of conceptually elliptical statements about freedom will
normally take the form indicated in the following schema:

$$\text{------ is free from ------}$$
$$\text{to do (or omit, or be, or have) ------.}$$

One fills in the first blank by naming the person (or persons) who is the
subject of the ascribed freedom, the second blank by specifying some compulsion or constraint, and the third blank by the specification of some action, omission, state of being, or possession actually or hypothetically desired
either by the subject or the speaker. (Note all the sources of ambiguity in
this formula!) If it is political freedom that is ascribed to the subject, then
the constraint will be coercion, and the fullest version of the statement
will specify not only the technique of constraint employed but also (in a
fourth blank) the identity of the coercers. Which blank in the schema is
the most important depends on the context in which a given statement is
made, and what is assumed to be understood by the persons addressed.

3. WHOSE FREEDOM?   There are occasions on which it is important to fill
                          in the first blank as clearly as any of the others.
This is especially true when persons uncritically use phrases which do not
mention the subjects of freedom, or slogans which conceal ambiguity by
the crude device of adding an adjective in qualification of the word "freedom." Maurice Cranston reminds us that both sides in the American Civil
War claimed (quite truly) to be fighting for "freedom," but the North
meant the freedom *of* slaves *from* their owners *to* go where they wished,
while the South meant the freedom *of* the states *from* the federal government *to* make their own laws. As for "freedom" as qualified by some
adjective, Cranston writes that "Conservatives, when they speak of 'economic freedom,' usually mean 'the freedom of the national economy from
the controls of the State.' Socialists advocating 'economic freedom' refer to
'the freedom of the individual from economic hardship.' "[11]

People who speak with rhetorical force and pretense to precision about
freedom as qualified by some adjective should always be invited to fill in
all the gaps in the schema. That is not to say that adjectival modifiers
cannot be useful, but only that they can be dangerous. We have already

[10] Cranston, *Freedom, A New Analysis*, p. 12.
[11] Cranston, *Freedom, A New Analysis*, pp. 13–14.

distinguished "political freedom" from freedom generally by the nature of the constraints that can restrict it; but "political freedom" might just as well be used to distinguish a certain range of actions—"political actions"— that might be impeded by restraints of any kind, or even a certain range of subjects—"political officials" or perhaps citizens—whose freedom is under discussion. The qualifying adjective, in short, might be taken as referring to any of the gaps in the schema, unless explicit directions are given for its interpretation.

4. POSITIVE AND NEGATIVE FREEDOM   It has often been said that there are two main concepts, or types, or ideals of freedom, one positive and the other negative, and that ideologies conflict insofar as they employ, or give emphasis to, one, the other, or both of them. Although writers who have attached great importance to this distinction have often gained important insights, their views can be preserved and expressed with greater economy in terms of the "single concept" analysis given here. The writers to whom I refer argue that only one of the two allegedly distinct concepts of freedom (the "negative") is to be analyzed as the absence of constraints.[12] We may be free of all constraints to our desire to do X, these philosophers maintain, and still not be free *to* do X. Hence, they conclude, "positive freedom" (freedom to . . .) is something other than the absence of constraint.

I think this way of indicating the distinction between positive and negative freedom will seem plausible only if the idea of a constraint is artificially limited. However, two important distinctions between kinds of constraints, cutting across each other, can be made, and once these distinctions are recognized, an apparent ground for the "two concept" analysis vanishes. The distinctions are those between positive and negative constraints and between internal and external constraints. There is no doubt that some constraints are negative—lack of money, strength, skill, or knowledge can quite effectively prevent a person from doing, or having, or being something he might want. Since these conditions are absences, they are "negative," and since they can be preventive causes, they are constraints.

How we make the distinction between "internal" and "external" constraints depends, of course, on how we draw the boundaries of the self. If we contract the self sufficiently so that it becomes a dimensionless nonempirical entity, then *all* causes are external. Other narrow conceptions of the self would attribute to its "inner core" a set of ultimate principles or

12 See Ralph Barton Perry, *Puritanism and Democracy* (New York: Vanguard Press, 1944), Chap. 18, and T. H. Green, *Lectures on Political Obligation* (London: Longmans, Green, and Co., 1901), especially the lecture on "Liberal Legislation and Freedom of Contract."

"internalized values," or ultimate ends or desires, and relegate to the merely "empirical self," or to a world altogether external to the self, all lower-ranked desires, whims, and fancies. If the distinction between internal and external constraints is to be put to *political* use, perhaps the simplest way of making it is by means of a merely spatial criterion: external constraints are those that come from outside a person's body-cum-mind, and all other constraints, whether sore muscles, headaches, or refractory "lower" desires, are internal to him. This would be to use a wide "total self," rather than the intimate "inner core" self, in making the distinction.

The two distinctions described above cut across one another, creating four categories. There are *internal positive constraints* such as headaches, obsessive thoughts, and compulsive desires; *internal negative constraints* such as ignorance, weakness, and deficiencies in talent or skill; *external positive constraints* such as barred windows, locked doors, and pointed bayonets; and *external negative constraints* such as lack of money, lack of transportation, and lack of weapons. Freedom from a negative constraint is the absence of an absence, and therefore the presence of some condition that permits a given kind of doing. When the presence of such a condition is external to a person, it is usually called an opportunity, and when internal, an ability. Not every absent condition whose presence would constitute an opportunity or ability, however, is a negative constraint. Only those whose absence constitutes a striking deviation from a norm of expectancy or propriety, or whose absence is in some way an important consideration for some practical interest either of the subject or of some later commentator, can qualify as constraints.

If only positive factors are counted as constraints, then a pauper might be free of constraints to his (actual or possible) desire to buy a Cadillac. But of course he is not free *to* buy a Cadillac. Similarly, if constraints are restricted to external factors, then the chronic alcoholic and the extremely ill man in a fever or coma are both free from constraints to go about their business; but of course, neither is free *to* do so. Once we acknowledge, however, that there can be internal and negative constraints, there is no further need to speak of two distinct kinds of freedom, one of which has nothing to do with constraint. A constraint is something—anything—that prevents one from doing something. Therefore, if nothing prevents me *from* doing X, I am free *to* do X; conversely, if I am free *to* do X, then nothing prevents me *from* doing X. "Freedom to" and "freedom from" are in this way logically linked, and there can be no special "positive" freedom *to* which is not also a freedom *from*.

Still, I suppose there is no harm in characterizing "positive freedom" as the absence of negative constraints, and "negative freedom" as the absence of positive constraints, *providing* (1) that positive and negative freedom are held to be equally necessary to a person's freedom all told (without any qualifying adjective), (2) neither is held to be "higher," "lower," or intrinsically more worth having than the other, and (3) neither is analyzed as totally different in kind from the absence of constraints.

5. SELF-RESTRAINT

Most of us do not *feel free* to perform acts that are forbidden by rules or authorities that we have accepted, even when there are no effective external hindrances and we stand to profit by disobedience. We are constrained from disobedience not by external barriers and threats but by internal inhibitions. Whether the internal constraint is taken to be a restriction of the self's freedom to act depends upon how we model the self, that is, upon which of the elements of the "total self" we identify most intimately with. If we are prevented by some internal element—an impulse, a craving, a weakened condition, an intense but illicit desire, a neurotic compulsion—from doing that which we think is the best thing to do, then the internal inhibitor is treated as an alien force, a kind of "enemy within." On the other hand, when the inhibitor is some higher-ranked desire and that which is frustrated is a desire of lesser importance albeit greater momentary intensity, we identify with the desire that is higher in our personal hierarchy, and consider ourselves to be the subject rather than the object of constraint. When the desire to do that which is forbidden is constrained by conscience, by the "internalized authority" of the prohibiting rules themselves, we identify with our consciences, and repel the threat to our personal integrity posed by the refractory lower desire which we "disown" no matter how "internal" it may be.

A person who had no hierarchical structure of wants, aims, and ideals, and no clear conception of where it is within his internal landscape that he really resides, would be a battlefield for all of his constituent elements, tugged this way and that, and fragmented hopelessly. Such a person would fail of autonomy not because he is a mere conformist whose values are all borrowed secondhand, for his wants, ideals, and scruples could be perfectly authentic and original in him, but because these values lack internal order and structure. This defective condition, which in its extreme form tends to be fatal, Durkheim called "anomie." It is interesting to note why, on the unitary "absence of constraint" theory of freedom, it is intelligible to speak of anomie as a kind of unfreedom. Our picture of the undisciplined or anomic man is not of a well-defined self with a literal or figurative bayonet at its back, or barriers, locked doors, and barred windows on all sides. Rather it employs the image of roads crowded with vehicles in the absence of traffic police or signals to keep order; desires, impulses, and purposes come and go at all speeds, in all directions, and get nowhere. The undisciplined person, perpetually liable to internal collisions, jams, and revolts, is unfree even though unrestrained by either the outside world or an internal governor. To vary the image, he is a person free of external shackles, but tied in knots by the strands of his own wants. In the apt current idiom, he is subject to "hang-ups." When he may "do anything he wants," his options will overwhelm his capacity to order them in hierarchies of preference. He will therefore become confused and disoriented, haunted by boredom and frustration, eager once more simply to be told what he must do. To be unfree is to be constrained, and in the absence of internal rules, desires will constrain each other in jams and collisions. Surely it is more plausible to construe such a state as unfreedom than as an illustration of the dreadfulness of too much freedom.

6. FREEDOM AS AUTONOMY

There is another use of the word "free," not yet mentioned, that provides still another—and a far more plausible—way of making a distinction between "positive" and "negative" kinds of freedom. This use has its primary and probably original[13] application not to individuals but to states and other institutions. Its inevitable extension to individual human beings was part of that elaborate parapolitical metaphor which since the time of Plato has so colored our conception of the human mind. To understand its extended use we would be well advised to consider first its literal application to states, which is a great deal clearer. When one nation is the colony of another, it is not said to be free until it gains its independence. Formerly, it was governed from without; now it is governed from within. Hence, freedom in this sense, and independence, and self-government all come to the same thing. Freedom in the sense of independence, as applied to states, does not at first seem to fit the unitary absence-of-constraint model (though it can be made to conform with a little tugging and pulling). The "free state" may be an impoverished tyranny with very little freedom for its citizens or for itself vis-à-vis other states and nature. Self-government might turn out to be even more repressive than foreign occupation. Yet, for all of that, the state might still be politically independent, sovereign, and governed from within, hence free.

Analogously, it is often said that the individual is "free" when his ruling part or "real self" governs, and is subject to no foreign power, either external or internal, to whose authority it has not consented. Suppose that John Doe wants nothing more than to have all his desires, actual and potential, free of constraints. He wants as many options as possible left open, especially those that are most important to him. He believes that Richard Roe knows best how to arrange this state of affairs. Hence, he puts himself under Roe's control, obeying as if commanded every piece of advice

[13] Lewis, *Studies in Words*, p. 112.

Roe gives him. The example becomes even more forceful if Doe makes this arrangement irrevocable. He is no longer self-determined, but receives rich dividends of satisfaction, having found a more effective way of getting all the particular things he wants or may one day come to want. (Self-direction is *not* one of the particular things he wants, nor is it important to him to keep open the option of one day repossessing it.) He may also want "breathing space" and "genuine options," in which case his benevolent director, Roe, arranges his life with these goals in mind. If this picture is coherent, the situation is analogous to that of the nation which gains freedom from constraint by becoming a colony of a wiser benevolent power. In each case, the subject can increase its freedom from constraint by relinquishing some of its power to govern itself. Both examples tend to show that self-government is a different kind of freedom from the absence of constraint.[14]

I think we can continue to speak of self-government as "freedom," however, without committing ourselves to the view that it is a kind of freedom unanalyzable in terms of the constraint model. Putatively distinct "concepts" of freedom frequently turn out to be different estimates of "the importance of only one part of what is always present in any case of freedom"[15]—the importance of one class of subjects as opposed to another, or of one class of desires or open options as opposed to another, or of one class of missing constraints as opposed to another. I think the point of calling individual self-direction *freedom* may be to emphasize the overriding importance of one particular kind of desire or option, namely, to decide for oneself what one shall do. Even wise and benevolent external direction is a constraint to the desire, actual or possible, to decide for oneself. Hence there is a point in calling the absence of *that* constraint (or the presence of self-direction) freedom.

In a similar way, almost anything can be made out as a constraint to *some* actual or possible desire. Hence the absence of anything at all (e.g., cloudy skies) can be identified with "true" or "positive" freedom. The point of singling out the desire to govern oneself for this special status is to acknowledge its supreme importance among desires. For those to whom the desire for self-government is so important that few other desires can yield significant satisfactions so long as it is constrained, there is every reason to preempt the word "freedom" for the absence of constraint to *it*. This singling out of a supreme desire is not a purely arbitrary or subjective thing. A powerful case can be made to show that other acknowledged values

14 Compare Berlin, *Two Concepts of Liberty*, p. 130: "The answer to the question—'Who governs me?'—is logically distinct from the question—'How far does government interfere with me?' It is in this difference that the great contrast between the two concepts of liberty in the end consists."
15 Gerald C. MacCallum, Jr., "Negative and Positive Freedom," *Philosophical Review*, LXXVI (1967), 318.

have self-government as their precondition, in particular that dignity, self-esteem, and responsibility are impossible without it.

7. PERMISSION AND ABILITY   One final distinction between types of constraints can obviate still other difficulties in interpreting singular judgments of the form "Doe is free *to* do *X*." A speaker might mean by this judgment either of the following:

1. *X* is something Doe *may* do, i.e., something he is *permitted* (but not required) to do by someone in authority over him, or by moral or legal rules to which he is subject. (Another way of saying this is that Doe is *at liberty* to do *X*.)
2. *X* is something that Doe *can* do, i.e., something he is *not in fact prevented* from doing (or required to do) either by coercion (direct or indirect) from others or by other kinds of constraints. (In this case, talk of "liberty" is not always interchangeable with talk of "freedom.")

When commands or rules are not effectively enforced, a person might well be able to do something that he is not permitted to do. Similarly, a person might be permitted to do something that he is unable to do because he is prevented by constraints other than rules backed by sanctions. A person might be also incapable of doing some act simply because it is prohibited by commands or rules that are effectively enforced. In that case, the enforced rule is itself a constraint.

Corresponding to the distinction between what *may* be done and what *can* be done is that between two perspectives from which singular freedom judgments are made, namely, the *juridical* and the *sociological*. The former is the perspective of a system of legal or legal-like regulations. When I say that no one in New York State is free to play poker for money in his own home, I am simply reciting what the New York legal codes prohibit. My judgment is confirmable or disconfirmable by reference to (and *only* by reference to) those codes. In fact, thousands of persons play poker for money in private homes in New York every night with little or no risk of apprehension by the indifferent police. When I speak from the sociological perspective, I might well say that everyone in New York is in effect free to play poker. This judgment is subject to a different kind of confirming or disconfirming evidence, including how effectively a law is enforced by the police, how intimidated by the law poker players actually feel, and how many of them are willing to run the risk of detection and conviction.

From the juridical perspective, what I am free to do in a given case is not a matter of degree. Any given act or omission is either permitted or it is not; I am at liberty (entirely) to do it or I am not at liberty to do it at all. Of course there are more subtle forms of legal control which employ variable constraints that permit talk of "degrees" of freedom. If there is a $100 tax on conduct of type *A* and a $500 tax on type *B,* I am left by authority, in a quite intelligible sense, more free to do *A* than to do *B.* In the case of criminal law, however, and all other regulations that control conduct by enjoining, permitting, and prohibiting, my freedom to do any act is, from the law's point of view, either entire or nonexistent. On the other hand, from the sociological perspective, it is always intelligible to speak of degrees of freedom or unfreedom even of a particular person to do some given act, and even when that act is unconditionally prohibited by law, if only because the probabilities of being detected and/or convicted vary from offense to offense.[16]

8. FREE ON BALANCE

A speaker may intend nothing so precise as is suggested by our schema with the three blanks when he asserts that he or some other person is free; but the second kind of thing he might mean presupposes and builds upon the singular noncomparative judgments discussed in this chapter. He may intend to convey that he is on the whole free, or at liberty, to do a great many things, or to do most of the things that are worth doing, or perhaps to do a greater percentage of the worthwhile things than are open to most people; or he might be emphasizing that he is free *from* most of the things that are worth being without in their own right (disease, poverty), or freer from those things than are the members of some comparison class. "On balance judgments" of freedom are of necessity vague and impressionistic, and even the comparative judgments that they sometimes incorporate are usually incapable of precise confirmation.

Suppose that John Doe is permitted by well-enforced rules to travel only to Chicago, Houston, and Seattle, but may make adverse criticism of nothing he sees in those cities, whereas Richard Roe may go only to Bridgeport, Elizabeth, and Jersey City and may criticize anything he wishes; or suppose that Doe can go anywhere at all but must not criticize, whereas Roe cannot leave home but may say anything he pleases. In reply to the question, "Which of the two is more free?" it appears that the only sensible answer is that Doe is more free in one respect (physical movement) and Roe in another (expression of opinion). If the questioner persists in asking who is the more free "on balance" and "in the last analysis," he must want to know which of the two respects is more important. If we are then to avoid a vitiating circularity, our standard of "importance" must be something other than "conducibility to freedom."

When two or more properties or "respects" are subject to precise mathematical comparison, they will always have some quantitative element in

[16] Cf. Felix Oppenheim, *Dimensions of Freedom* (New York: St. Martin's Press, Inc., 1961), p. 187.

common. The difficulty in striking resultant totals of "on balance freedom" derives from the fact that the relation among the various "areas" in which people are said to be free is not so much like the relation between the height, breadth, and depth of a physical object as it is like the relation between the gasoline economy, styling, and comfort of an automobile.[17] Height times breadth times depth equals volume, a dimension compounded coherently out of the others; freedom of expression times freedom of movement yields nothing comparable. If these areas of freedom are called "dimensions," they must also be labeled "incommensurable." Still, limited comparisons even of incommensurables are possible. If the average American has greater freedom in *every* dimension than his Ruritanian counterpart, it makes sense to say that he has greater freedom on balance; if they are equally free in some dimensions but the American is more free in all the others, the same judgment follows. What we more likely mean when we say that one subject is freer on balance than another is that his freedom is greater in the more valuable, important, or significant dimensions, where the "value" of a dimension is determined by some independent standard.

A result of considerable interest seems to follow from this analysis. Since "maximal freedom" (having as much freedom on balance as possible) is a notion that makes sense only through the application of independent standards for determining the relative worth or importance of different sorts of interests and areas of activity, it is by itself a merely formal ideal that cannot stand on its own feet without the help of other values. One person's freedom can conflict with another's, freedom in one dimension can contrast with freedom in another, and the conflicting dimensions cannot meaningfully be combined on one scale. These conflicts and recalcitrances require that we put types of subjects, possible desires, and areas of activity into some order of importance; this in turn requires supplementing the political ideal of freedom with moral standards of other kinds. The supplementary values, however, are not external to freedom in the manner of such independently conceived rival ideals as justice and welfare, but rather are "internally supplementary"—a necessary filling-in of the otherwise partially empty idea of "on balance freedom" itself.

17 Cf. Oppenheim, *Dimensions of Freedom*, p. 200.

CHAPTER TWO

Grounds
for Coercion

1. THE PRESUMPTIVE CASE FOR LIBERTY   Whatever else we believe about freedom, most of us believe it is something to be praised, or so luminously a Thing of Value that it is beyond praise. What is it that makes freedom a good thing? Some say that freedom is good in itself quite apart from its consequences. On the other hand, James Fitzjames Stephen wrote that "...the question whether liberty is a good or a bad thing appears as irrational as the question whether fire is a good or a bad thing."[1] Freedom, according to Stephen, is good (when it is good) only because of what it does, not because of what it is.

It would be impossible to demonstrate that freedom is good for its own sake, and indeed, this proposition is far from self-evident. Still, Stephen's analogy to fire seems an injustice to freedom. Fire has no constant and virtually invariant effects that tend to make it, on balance, a good thing whenever and wherever it occurs, and bad only when its subsequent remoter effects are so evil as to counterbalance its direct and immediate ones. Thus, a fire in one's bed while one is sleeping is dreadful because its

[1] James Fitzjames Stephen, *Liberty, Equality, Fraternity* (London: 1873), p. 48.

effects are evil, but a fire under the pot on the stove is splendid because it makes possible a hot cup of coffee when one wants it. The direct effect of fire in these and all other cases is to oxidize material objects and raise the temperature in its immediate environment; but *these* effects, from the point of view of human interests, and considered just in themselves, are neither good nor bad.

Freedom has seemed to most writers quite different in this respect. When a free man violates his neighbor's interests, then his freedom, having been put to bad use, was, on balance, a bad thing, but unlike the fire in the bed, it was not an unalloyed evil. Whatever the harmful consequences of freedom in a given case, there is always a direct effect on the person of its possessor which must be counted a positive good. Coercion may prevent great evils, and be wholly justified on that account, but it always has its price. Coercion may be on balance a great gain, but its direct effects always, or nearly always, constitute a definite loss. If this is true, there is always a *presumption* in favor of freedom, even though it can in some cases be overridden by more powerful reasons on the other side.

The presumption in favor of freedom is usually said to rest on freedom's essential role in the development of traits of intellect and character which constitute the good of individuals and are centrally important means to the progress of societies. One consensus argument, attributable with minor variations to Von Humboldt, Mill, Hobhouse, and many others, goes roughly as follows. The highest good for man is neither enjoyment, nor passive contentment, but rather a dynamic process of growth and self-realization. This can be called "happiness" if we mean by that term what the Greeks did, namely, "The exercise of vital powers along lines of excellence in a life affording them scope."[2] The highest social good is then the greatest possible amount of individual self-realization and (assuming that different persons are inclined by their natures in different ways) the resultant diversity and fullness of life. Self-realization consists in the actualization of certain uniquely human potentialities, the bringing to full development of certain powers and abilities. This in turn requires constant practice in making difficult choices among alternative hypotheses, policies, and actions—and the more difficult the better. John Stuart Mill explained why:

The human faculties of perception, judgment, discriminative feeling, mental activity, and even moral preference are exercised only in making a choice. He who does anything because it is the custom makes no choice. He gains no practice either in discerning or in desiring what is best. The mental and moral, like the muscular, powers are improved only by being used.[3]

In short, one does not realize what is best in oneself when social pressures

2 See Edith Hamilton, *The Greek Way* (New York: W. W. Norton & Company, Inc., 1942), pp. 35 ff.
3 John Stuart Mill, *On Liberty* (New York: Liberal Arts Press, 1956), p. 71.

to conform to custom lead one mindlessly along. Even more clearly, one's growth will be stunted when one is given no choice in the first place, either because of being kept in ignorance or because one is terrorized by the wielders of bayonets.

Freedom to decide on one's own while fully informed of the facts thus tends to promote the good of the person who exercises it, even if it permits him to make foolish or dangerous mistakes. Mill added to this argument the citation of numerous social benefits that redound indirectly but uniformly to those who grant freedom as well as those who exercise it. We all profit from the fruits of genius, he maintained, and genius, since it often involves doggedness and eccentricity, is likely to flourish only where coercive pressures toward conformity are absent. Moreover, social progress is more likely to occur where there is free criticism of prevailing ways and adventurous experiments in living. Finally, true understanding of human nature requires freedom, since without liberty there will be little diversity, and without diversity *all* aspects of the human condition will be ascribed to fixed nature rather than to the workings of a particular culture.

Such are the grounds for holding that there is always a presumption in favor of freedom, that whenever we are faced with an option between forcing a person to do something and letting him decide on his own whether or not to do it, other things being equal, we should always opt for the latter. If a strong general presumption for freedom has been established, the burden of proof rests on the shoulders of the advocate of coercion, and the philosopher's task will be to state the conditions under which the presumption can be overridden.

2. THE ANARCHISTIC PRINCIPLE   It will be instructive to see why certain very simple statements of the conditions for justified social and political coercion are unsatisfactory. The first of these, which might with propriety be called "anarchistic," insists that society and the state should grant to every citizen "complete liberty to do whatever he wishes." In this view, no coercive power exercised by state or society is ever justified. What then of the coercion imposed by one individual or group on another? If every man is free to do whatever he wishes, it follows that all men are free to inflict blows on John Doe, to hold noisy parties under his window every night, and to help themselves to his possessions. How can it then be true that John Doe is free at the same time to come and go as he pleases, to sleep at night, and to enjoy exclusive use of his possessions?

There is no *logical* inconsistency in holding both that Doe is dispositionally free to do something and that someone else, Roe, is dispositionally free to prevent him from doing that thing. (I am considering these judgments only when made from the sociological, not the juridical, perspective.)

Consider the statements that Doe is free to go to Chicago and Roe is free to keep Doe from going anywhere. It would be something of an over-simplification, but useful for our present purposes, to regard these statements as equivalent to the following hypotheticals: (1) If Doe chooses to go to Chicago, he will in fact go to Chicago, and (2) If Roe chooses to have Doe stay at home, Doe will in fact stay at home. There are conceivable circumstances in which both of these statements would be true. One set of facts that would make them both true would be those obtaining when Roe has the power to prevent Doe from leaving home, but does *not* choose to exercise that power, and no other obstacle stands in Doe's way. Thus, (1) is true because if, in these circumstances, Doe chooses to go to Chicago, there is nothing to stop him; (2) is true because if (contrary to fact) Roe were to choose to keep Doe at home, Doe would be kept at home. For any Doe and any Roe, whether or not (1) and (2) are true together depends upon what the facts happen to be. The conjunction of (1) and (2), therefore, cannot be logically contradictory.

There is no logical barrier to its being true that *everyone* is free (from coercion) to do whatever he may choose. One can conceive of logically possible worlds in which this would be the case. But in order for it to be true of our actual world, there would have to be a disappearance of conflict between choices: as soon as two men attempt to acquire what only one can have, or one man desires something that can be acquired only by frustrating the desires of someone else, then one man's freedom is possible only at the cost of another man's constraint. The anarchistic principle, in short, would be workable only in a world in which human desires and choices, through a miracle of preestablished harmony, could never conflict. In our own world, where conflict and rivalry are ineradicable facts, "complete liberty for all" on the anarchist formula would mean greater freedom for the strong than the weak, and no very stable freedoms for anyone.

Given that the important desires of men can and usually do conflict, one person will be free to act on a desire only to the extent that others are unfree to act on conflicting desires; if the state is to guarantee to all men the freedom to do one certain kind of thing, then, in all likelihood, it must make all men unfree to prevent others from doing that sort of thing. "As against the coercion applicable by individual to individual," wrote Bentham, "no liberty can be given to one man but in proportion as it is taken away from another. All coercive laws, therefore, and in particular all laws creative of liberty, are as far as they go abrogative of liberty."[4] But if prohibitive laws destroy a liberty for every liberty they confer or protect, while the anarchistic principle would neither add nor subtract liberties from the natural situation of men, don't they yield precisely the

4 Jeremy Bentham, "Anarchical Fallacies," in *The Works of Jeremy Bentham*, Vol. 2, ed. John Bowring (Edinburgh, 1843).

same net totals of liberty and constraint, differing merely in the manner of distribution? This conclusion is yet another trap we can fall into by interpreting usefully loose talk about "amounts" of freedom in a precise quantitative way.

Most civilized societies have prohibitive laws or other social devices to prevent individuals from inflicting blows on the faces of other individuals. There is sometimes a great deal of pleasure to be derived from bopping someone in the nose, but most of us think that this pleasure is worth sacrificing for the greater good of security from physical attack by others. Suppose, however, that some rugged individualist complains that our law infringes on his freedom, making it virtually impossible for him to enjoy the thrill of smashing noses, and just because of the scruples of a lot of weak-kneed, lily-livered sissies. "Since the days of the frontier," he might say, "there hasn't been any real freedom in this country." We should no doubt try to explain to him that the interest people have in the physical integrity of their noses is *more important* than their aggressive interests, and therefore more worthy of protection.

Now suppose that we had quite different rules, and that more people were free to hit others in the nose, and correspondingly fewer were free to enjoy the full beauty and utility of their own unbloodied proboscises. Would this new arrangement have a greater or smaller "amount" of freedom in it, on balance? Perhaps it is least misleading to say that there would be not "less" freedom but freedom of a morally inferior kind. Most societies have recognized that there are some relatively permanent desires present in all men that must be singled out, given precedence, and made legally sacrosanct. When these interests are so recognized and protected by law, they come to be called *rights* (see Chapter 4). Selection of those interests important enough to be protected in this way is made in accordance with the settled value judgments of the community by application of some standard other than that of "simple freedom" itself, which is quite insufficient. To receive "complete liberty" from society and its government would be to incur other constraints from private individuals, and almost all who have thought about this exchange consider it a bad trade.

3. THE FORMALISTIC PRINCIPLE   The second unsatisfactory principle of freedom distribution does not have such obvious failings. In fact, many have spoken as if it were a self-evident truth. Society, it says, should grant to every person "full liberty to do what he pleases providing only that he does not interfere with the like liberty of another."[5] This principle is the right answer to the wrong question. It

[5] L. T. Hobhouse, *The Elements of Social Justice* (London: George Allen & Unwin Ltd., 1922), p. 60. Hobhouse rejects this formula, and I have adapted his argument against it in the text.

insists that liberty should be distributed impartially, and that no individual take exception to the general prohibitive laws. But if it is taken as an answer to our question—when is political or social coercion justified?—it is entirely formal and empty, and consistent with any system of legal constraints that is not arbitrary. A general rule permitting nose-bopping would satisfy it just as well as one prohibiting it; the anarchistic principle conforms to it, as well as a principle prohibiting all aggressive behavior. The principle employs a sound maxim of justice, insisting as it does on nondiscriminatory legislation and impartial enforcement, but it provides no guide to the proper *content* of the law. Its inadequacy as a substantive principle of freedom distribution was well appreciated by L. T. Hobhouse, who wrote, "My right to keep my neighbor awake by playing the piano all night is not satisfactorily counterbalanced by his right to keep a dog which howls all the time the piano is being played."[6] Each party in this example would use his freedom to the detriment of the other under a law which recognizes a "like liberty" for the other party to do the same if he can. That the law is nondiscriminatory would be small consolation to either party if it permitted his interests to be seriously harmed.

4. THE CONCEPT OF HARM   If social and political coercion is a harm-causing evil, then one way to justify it is to show that it is necessary for the prevention of even greater evils. That is the generating insight of the "harm to others principle" (henceforth called simply "the harm principle") which permits society to restrict the liberty of some persons in order to prevent harm to others. Two versions of this principle can be distinguished. The first would justify restriction of one person's liberty to prevent injury to other specific individuals, and can therefore be called "the private harm principle." The second can be invoked to justify coercion on the distinct ground that it is necessary to prevent impairment of institutional practices and regulatory systems that are in the public interest; thus it can be called "the public harm principle." That the private harm principle (whose chief advocate was J. S. Mill) states at least one of the acceptable grounds for coercion is virtually beyond controversy. Hardly anyone would deny the state the right to make criminal such directly injurious conduct as willful homicide, assault and battery, and robbery. Mill often wrote as if prevention of private harm is the *sole* valid ground for state coercion, but this must not have been his considered intention. He would not have wiped from the books such crimes as tax evasion, smuggling, and contempt of court, which need not injure any specific individuals, except insofar as they weaken public institutions in whose health we all

6 L. T. Hobhouse, *Liberalism* (New York: Holt, Rinehart and Winston, Inc., 1911), pp. 63–64.

have a stake. I shall assume that Mill held both the public and private versions of the harm principle.

In its simplest formulations, the harm principle is still a long way from being a precise guide to the ideal legislator, especially in those difficult cases where harms of different orders, magnitudes, and probabilities must be balanced against one another. Even when made fully explicit and qualified in appropriate ways, however, the unsupplemented harm principle cannot be fairly assessed until it is known precisely what is meant by "harm."

(i) HARM AS THE INVASION OF AN INTEREST

It has become common, especially in legal writings, to take the object of harm always to be an *interest*. The *Restatement of the Law of Torts* gives one sense of the term "interest" when it defines it as "anything which is the object of human desire,"[7] but this seems much too broad to be useful for our present purposes. A person is often said to "have an interest" in something he does not presently desire. A dose of medicine may be "in a man's interest" even when he is struggling and kicking to avoid it. In this sense, an object of an interest is "what is truly good for a person whether he desires it or not." Even interest defined in this second way may be indirectly but necessarily related to desires. The only way to argue that X is in Doe's interest even though Doe does not want X may be to show that X would effectively integrate Doe's total set of desires leading to a greater net balance of desire-fulfillment in the long run. If most of Doe's acknowledged important desires cannot be satisfied so long as he is ill, and he cannot become well unless he takes the medicine, then taking the medicine is in Doe's interest in this desire-related sense.

Legal writers classify interests in various ways. One of the more common lists "Interests of Personality," "Interests of Property," "Interest in Reputation," "Interest in Domestic Relations," and "Interest in Privacy," among others. A humanly inflicted harm is conceived as the violation of one of a person's interests, an injury to something in which he has a genuine stake. In the lawyer's usage, an interest is something a person always possesses in some condition, something that can grow and flourish or diminish and decay, but which can rarely be totally lost. Other persons can be said to promote or hinder an individual's interest in bodily health, or in the avoidance of damaging or offensive physical contacts, or in the safety and security of his person, his family, his friends, and his property. One advantage of this mode of speaking is that it permits us to appraise harms by distinguishing between more and less important interests, and between those interests which are, and those which are not, worthy of legal recognition and/or protection.

[7] *Restatement of the Law of Torts* (St. Paul: American Law Institute, 1939), p. 1.

(ii) HARM VS. HURT: THE ROLE OF KNOWLEDGE

Is it true that "what a person doesn't know can't *harm* him"? For most cases, this maxim certainly does *not* apply, and it is one of the merits of the "interest" analysis of harm that it explains why. Typically, having one's interests violated is one thing, and knowing that one's interests have been violated is another. The rich man is harmed at the time his home is burgled, even though he may not discover the harm for months; similarly, a soldier is harmed the moment he is wounded, though in the heat of the battle he may not discover even his serious wounds for some time. The law does not permit a burglar to plead "He will never miss it" even when that plea is true, for the crime of burglary consists in inflicting a forbidden harm, whether or not it will be discovered or will hurt. It is true that not all harms *hurt,* partly because not all harms ever come to be noticed. There may well be a relatively narrow and precise sense of "harm" in ordinary usage such that "being harmed" can be contrasted with being hurt (as well as with "being shocked" and "being offended"). However, if harm is understood as the violation of an interest, and all men have an interest in not being hurt, it follows that hurt is one species of harm. Hence, even though not all harms hurt, all hurts do harm (or more accurately, are themselves harm), and the harm principle could conceivably be used to justify coercion when it is necessary to prevent hurts, even when the hurts do not lead to any *further* harm.

There are some special cases where the maxim "What a person doesn't know can't *hurt* him" seems quite sound. In these cases, knowledge of some fact, such as the adulterous infidelities of one's spouse, is itself hurtful; indeed, the whole hurt consists in the knowledge and is inseparable from it. Here knowledge is both a necessary and sufficient condition of a hurt: What the cuckolded husband doesn't know "can't hurt him." That is not to say that he cannot be *harmed* unless he is hurt. An undetected adultery damages one of the victim's "interests in domestic relations," just as an unknown libelous publication can damage his interest in a good reputation, or an undetected trespass on his land can damage his interest in "the exclusive enjoyment and control" of that land. In all these cases, violation of the interest in question is itself a harm even though no *further* harm may result to any other interests.

The distinction between hurt and (generic) harm raises one additional question. We must include in the category of "hurts" not only physical pains but also forms of mental distress. Our question is whether, in applying the harm principle, we should permit coercion designed to prevent mental distress when the distress is not likely to be followed by hurt or harm of any other kind. Some forms of mental distress (e.g., "hurt feelings") can be ruled out simply on the ground that they are too minor or trivial to warrant interference. Others are so severe that they can lead to mental breakdowns. In such cases, however, it is the consequential harm to mental health and not the mere fact of distress that clearly warrants interference on the ground of harmfulness. Thus, a convenient criterion for determining whether a hurt is sufficiently harmful to justify preventive coercion on that ground suggests itself: the hurt is serious enough if and only if it is either a symptom of a prior or concurrent harm of another order (as a pain in an arm may be the result and sign of a broken bone), or is in itself the cause of a consequential harm (e.g., mental breakdown) of another order.

(iii) HARM VS. OFFENSE

The relation of offensiveness to harmfulness can be treated in much the same way as that of hurtfulness to harmfulness. The following points can be made of both:

1. Some harms do not offend (as some do not hurt).
2. All offenses (like all hurts) are harms, inasmuch as all men have an interest in not being offended or hurt.
3. Some offenses (like some hurts) are symptoms or consequences of prior or concurrent harms.
4. Some offenses (like some hurts) are causes of subsequent harms: in the case of extreme hurt, harm to health; in the case of extreme offense, harm from provoked ill will or violence. These subsequent harms are harms of a different order, i.e., violations of interests other than the interest in not being hurt or offended.
5. Some offenses, like some hurts, are "harmless," i.e., do not lead to any *further* harm (violations of any interests other than the interest in not being hurt or offended).
6. Although offense and hurt are in themselves harms, they are harms of a relatively trivial kind (unless they are of sufficient magnitude to violate interests in health and peace).

Partly because of points 5 and 6, many writers use the word "harm" in a sense that is much narrower than "the invasion of any interest." In this narrower sense, harm is distinguished from and even contrasted with "mere offense." Some distinguish "harm to one's interests" from "offense to one's feelings" (as if there were no interest in unoffended feelings). This is a permissible, even useful, way of talking, if we agree that offensiveness as such is strictly speaking a kind of harm, but harm of such a trivial kind that it cannot by itself ever counterbalance the direct and immediate harm caused by coercion. One should appreciate how radical the harm principle is when interpreted in the strict and narrow way that excludes mere offensiveness as a relevant sort of harm. Both the British Wolfenden Report and the American Model Penal Code, for example, recognize "harmless" offensiveness as a ground for preventive coercion in some circumstances (see Chapter 3). For clarity and convenience only, I shall stipulate then that "offensiveness as such" is a proposed ground for coercion distinct from harm of the sort required by the harm principle (narrowly interpreted), so that "the offense principle" can be treated as an independent principle in its own right.

Offensive behavior is such in virtue of its capacity to induce in others any of a large miscellany of mental states that have little in common except that they are unpleasant, uncomfortable, or disliked. These states do not necessarily "hurt," as do sorrow and distress. Rather the relation between them and hurt is analogous to that between physical unpleasantness and pain, for there is also a great miscellany of unpleasant but not painful bodily states—itches, shocks, and discomforts—that have little in common except that they don't hurt but are nevertheless universally disliked. Among the main sorts of "harmless but disliked" *mental* states are irritating sensations (e.g., bad smells, cacophony, clashing colors), disgust, shocked moral sensibilities, and shameful embarrassment.

(iv) HARM VS. NONBENEFIT

When the harm principle is unsupplemented by any other accepted ground for coercion, it decrees that state power may not be used against one person to *benefit* another, but only to prevent harm to another. One way of coercing citizens is to force them to pay taxes in support of various state activities. A partisan of the harm principle might be expected to cast a suspicious eye on all such schemes of involuntary support. Indeed, he might argue that taxing some to educate others is to coerce some merely to benefit others, or that taxing some to provide libraries, museums, theatres, or concert halls for others is to coerce some merely to amuse, inspire, or edify others, and is therefore unjustified.[8] On the other hand, an advocate of the harm principle could with consistency *deny* the foregoing propositions if he had a different way of construing the harm-nonbenefit distinction.

One muddled way of basing the distinction between harms and mere nonbenefits is to make it correspond to that between acting and omitting to act to another's detriment.[9] That will not do for the obvious reason that it is possible to harm or to benefit another either by action or omission. In other words, both actions and omissions can be the *cause* of changes in another's condition for better or worse. If we judge that Doe's failure to save the drowning swimmer Roe was the cause of Roe's death, then we can label Doe's omission the mere "withholding of a benefit" only if we judge the loss of life itself, in the circumstances, to be the loss of a benefit rather than the incurring of a harm. If, on the other hand, loss of one's life, like loss of one's health, fortune, or loved ones, is itself a harm, then anything that causes such a loss, whether it be act, omission, or fortuitous event, causes a harm.

8 Cf. Stephen, *Liberty, Equality, Fraternity,* p. 16.
9 See, for example, James Barr Ames, "Law and Morals," *Harvard Law Review,* XXII (1908), pp. 97–113, and Lord Macaulay, "Notes on the Indian Penal Code," *Works* (London: Longmans, Green & Co. Ltd., 1866), Vol. VII, p. 497.

Another unsatisfactory way of basing the harm-nonbenefit distinction is to hold that being without something good is a mere nonbenefit, whereas being in possession of something evil is a harm. It would follow from such a view that not learning truths is not having a good and hence not being benefited, whereas being told lies is to be in possession of something bad, and is therefore to be harmed. Thus it would follow that education is a mere benefit and its lack no harm. But surely this will not do. To be effectively deprived of all food is clearly to be harmed as much as to be given poisoned food; the upshot in each case is death. Similarly, to have hardly any knowledge of the world is to be handicapped so severely as to be harmed, though perhaps not as severely as to have imposed on one a systematic set of falsehoods. In either case the result is damage to one's vital interests. Harm, therefore, is no more linked to "positive" possessions than it is to "positive" actions. It can consist in a lack as well as a presence, just as it can be caused by an omission as well as an action.

More promising correlations, at first sight, are those between harms and unmet *needs* and between benefits and unneeded goods. We harm a man when we deny or deprive him of something he needs; we fail to benefit him (merely) when we deny or deprive him of some good he does not need. An unneeded good is something a person wants which is not necessary for his welfare, something he can do without. To receive something one wants but does not need is to benefit or profit, but not to the point where loss of the gain would be a harm. Thus, if I have an annual salary of one hundred thousand dollars, and my employer gives me a fifty thousand dollar raise, I benefit substantially from his largesse. If he fails to give me a raise, I am not so benefited, but surely not harmed either (given my needs). If he reduces me to five thousand or fires me, however, he not merely fails to benefit me, he causes me harm by withholding money I *need*. These examples suggest that a statesman or legislator who is committed to an unsupplemented harm principle must have means for distinguishing authentic human needs from mere wants, and that his problem is little different in principle from that of the ordinary householder who must often distinguish between "luxuries" and "necessities" when he plans his household budget.

The problem is more complex, however, than these homey examples suggest. The "unmet need" analysis of harm would imply, for example, that a rich man is not harmed by a minor larceny, a conclusion we have already rejected. Still another distinction can be helpful at this point: that between *being in a harmful condition* (whatever its cause or origin) and undergoing *a change in one's condition in a harmful direction*. To deprive even a rich man of money is to damage his interests, that is, to change his condition for the worse, even though not yet to the state of actual injury. Thus, it is to "harm" him in one sense, but not in another. At best, the

"unmet need" criterion is a test for determining when a damaged interest
has reached the threshold of "actual injury," rather than a weathervane-
indicator of harmful directions. Let us stipulate at this point, for the sake
of clarity and convenience, that the harm principle be interpreted in such
a way that changes in the condition of a protectable interest in harmful
directions, even short of the stage of "actual injury" (unmet need), count
as a kind of harm, the prevention of which, in some circumstances, may
justify coercion. However, when harms have to be ranked and balanced
in a given application of the harm principle, an actually injurious condition
should outweigh a mere change in a harmful direction.

5. LINES OF ATTACK ON MILL

Arguments against Mill's unsupplemented harm principle (his claim that the private and public harm
principles state the *only* grounds for justified interference with liberty) have been mainly of two different kinds.[10] Many have
argued that the harm principle justifies too much social and political interference in the affairs of individuals. Others allow that the prevention of
individual and social harm is always a ground for interference, but insist
that it is by no means the only ground.

(i) "NO MAN IS AN ISLAND"

Mill maintained in *On Liberty* that social interference is never justified
in those of a man's affairs that concern himself only. But no man's affairs
have effects on himself alone. There are a thousand subtle and indirect
ways in which every individual act, no matter how private and solitary,
affects others. It would therefore seem that society has a right, on Mill's
own principles, to interfere in every department of human life. Mill anticipated this objection and took certain steps to disarm it. Let it be allowed
that no human conduct is entirely, exclusively, and to the last degree self-
regarding. Still, Mill insisted, we can distinguish between actions that are
plainly other-regarding and those that are "directly," "chiefly," or "primarily" self-regarding. There will be a twilight area of cases difficult to
classify, but that is true of many other workable distinctions, including
that between night and day.

It is essential to Mill's theory that we make a distinction between two
different kinds of consequences of human actions: the consequences *directly*
affecting the interests of others, and those of primarily self-regarding behavior which only *indirectly* or *remotely* affect the interests of others. "No
person ought to be punished simply for being drunk," Mill wrote, "but a

10 Cf. H. L. A. Hart, *Law, Liberty, and Morality* (Stanford: Stanford University
Press, 1963), p. 5.

soldier or policeman should be punished for being drunk on duty."[11] A drunk policeman directly harms the interests of others. His conduct gives opportunities to criminals and thus creates grave risk of harm to other citizens. It brings the police into disrepute, and makes the work of his colleagues more dangerous. Finally, it may lead to loss of the policeman's job, with serious consequences for his wife and children.

Consider, on the other hand, a hard working bachelor who habitually spends his evening hours drinking himself into a stupor, which he then sleeps off, rising fresh in the morning to put in another hard day's work. His drinking does not *directly* affect others in any of the ways of the drunk policeman's conduct. He has no family; he drinks alone and sets no direct example; he is not prevented from discharging any of his public duties; he creates no substantial risk of harm to the interests of other individuals. Although even his private conduct will have some effects on the interests of others, these are precisely the sorts of effects Mill would call "indirect" and "remote." First, in spending his evenings the way he does, our solitary tippler is *not* doing any number of other things that might be of greater utility to others. In not earning and spending more money, he is failing to stimulate the economy (except for the liquor industry) as much as he might. Second, he fails to spend his evening time improving his talents and making himself a better person. Perhaps he has a considerable native talent for painting or poetry, and his wastefulness is depriving the world of some valuable art. Third, he may make those of his colleagues who like him sad on his behalf. Finally, to those who know of his habits, he is a "bad example."[12] All of these "indirect harms" together, Mill maintained, do not outweigh the direct and serious harm that would result from social or legal coercion.

Mill's critics have never been entirely satisfied by this. Many have pointed out that Mill is concerned not only with political coercion and legal punishment but also with purely social coercion—moral pressure, social avoidance, ostracism. No responsible critic would wish the state to punish the solitary tippler, but social coercion is another matter. We can't prevent people from disapproving of an individual for his self-regarding faults or from expressing that disapproval to others, without undue restriction on *their* freedom. Such expressions, in Mill's view, are inevitably coercive, constituting a "milder form of punishment." Hence "social punishment" of individuals for conduct that directly concerns only themselves—the argument concludes—is both inevitable and, according to Mill's own principles, proper.

11 Mill, *On Liberty*, pp. 99–100.

12 Mill has a ready rejoinder to this last point: If the conduct in question is supposed to be greatly harmful to the actor himself, "the example, on the whole must be more salutory" than harmful socially, since it is a warning lesson, rather than an alluring model, to others. See Mill, *On Liberty*, p. 101.

Mill anticipated this objection, too, and tried to cope with it by making a distinction between types of social responses. We cannot help but lower in our estimation a person with serious self-regarding faults. We will think ill of him, judge him to be at fault, and make him the inevitable and proper object of our disapproval, distaste, even contempt. We may warn others about him, avoid his company, and withhold gratuitous benefits from him—"not to the oppression of his individuality but in the exercise of ours."[13] Mill concedes that all of these social responses can function as "penalties"—but they are suffered "only in so far as they are the natural and, as it were, the spontaneous consequences of the faults themselves, not because they are purposely inflicted on him for the sake of punishment."[14] Other responses, on the other hand, add something to the "natural penalties"—pointed snubbing, economic reprisals, gossip campaigns, and so on. The added penalties, according to Mill, are precisely the ones that are never justified as responses to merely self-regarding flaws—"if he displeases us, we may express our distaste; and we may stand aloof from a person as well as from a thing that displeases us, but we shall not therefore feel called on to make his life uncomfortable."[15]

(ii) OTHER PROPOSED GROUNDS FOR COERCION

The distinction between self-regarding and other-regarding behavior, as Mill intended it to be understood, does seem at least roughly serviceable, and unlikely to invite massive social interference in private affairs. I think most critics of Mill would grant that, but reject the harm principle on the opposite ground that it doesn't permit enough interference. These writers would allow at least one, and as many as five or more, additional valid grounds for coercion. Each of these proposed grounds is stated in a principle listed below. One might hold that restriction of one person's liberty can be justified:

1. To prevent harm to others, either
   a. injury to individual persons (*The Private Harm Principle*), or
   b. impairment of institutional practices that are in the public interest (*The Public Harm Principle*);
2. To prevent offense to others (*The Offense Principle*);
3. To prevent harm to self (*Legal Paternalism*);
4. To prevent or punish sin, i.e., to "enforce morality as such" (*Legal Moralism*);
5. To benefit the self (*Extreme Paternalism*);
6. To benefit others (*The Welfare Principle*).

The liberty-limiting principles on this list are best understood as stating neither necessary nor sufficient conditions for justified coercion, but rather specifications of the *kinds* of reasons that are always relevant or acceptable

[13] Mill, *On Liberty*, p. 94.
[14] Mill, *On Liberty*, p. 95.
[15] Mill, *On Liberty*, p. 96.

in support of proposed coercion, even though in a given case they may not be conclusive.[16] Each principle states that interference might be permissible *if* (but not *only if*) a certain condition is satisfied. Hence the principles are not mutually exclusive; it is possible to hold two or more of them at once, even all of them together, and it is possible to deny all of them. Moreover, the principles cannot be construed as stating sufficient conditions for legitimate interference with liberty, for even though the principle is satisfied in a given case, the general presumption against coercion might not be outweighed. The harm principle, for example, does not justify state interference to prevent a tiny bit of inconsequential harm. Prevention of minor harm always counts in favor of proposals (as in a legislature) to restrict liberty, but in a given instance it might not count *enough* to outweigh the general presumption against interference, or it might be outweighed by the prospect of practical difficulties in enforcing the law, excessive costs, and forfeitures of privacy. A liberty-limiting principle states considerations that are always good reasons for coercion, though neither exclusively nor, in every case, decisively good reasons.

It will not be possible to examine each principle in detail here, and offer "proofs" and "refutations." The best way to defend one's selection of principles is to show to which positions they commit one on such issues as censorship of literature, "morals offenses," and compulsory social security programs. General principles arise in the course of deliberations over particular problems, especially in the efforts to defend one's judgments by showing that they are consistent with what has gone before. If a principle commits one to an antecedently unacceptable judgment, then one has to modify or supplement the principle in a way that does the least damage to the harmony of one's particular and general opinions taken as a group. On the other hand, when a solid, well-entrenched principle entails a change in a particular judgment, the overriding claims of consistency may require that the judgment be adjusted. This sort of dialectic is similar to the reasonings that are prevalent in law courts. When similar cases are decided in opposite ways, it is incumbent on the court to distinguish them in some respect that will reconcile the separate decisions with each other and with the common rule applied to each. Every effort is made to render current decisions consistent with past ones unless the precedents seem so disruptive of the overall internal harmony of the law that they must, reluctantly, be revised or abandoned. In social and political philosophy every person is on his own, and the counterparts to "past decisions" are the most confident judgments one makes in ordinary normative discourse. The philosophical task is to extract from these "given" judgments the principles

---

[16] I owe this point to Professor Michael Bayles. See his contribution to *Issues in Law and Morality*, ed. Norman Care and Thomas Trelogan (Cleveland: The Press of Case Western Reserve University, 1973).

that render them consistent, adjusting and modifying where necessary in order to convert the whole body of opinions into an intelligible, coherent system. There is no a priori way of refuting another's political opinions, but if our opponents are rational men committed to the ideal of consistency, we can always hope to show them that a given judgment is inconsistent with one of their own acknowledged principles. Then something will have to give.

CHAPTER THREE

Hard Cases for the Harm Principle

1. MORALS OFFENSES AND LEGAL MORALISM Immoral conduct is no trivial thing, and we should hardly expect societies to tolerate it; yet if men are *forced* to refrain from immorality, their own choices will play very little role in what they do, so that they can hardly develop critical judgment and moral traits of a genuinely praiseworthy kind. Thus legal enforcement of morality seems to pose a dilemma. The problem does not arise if we assume that all immoral conduct is socially harmful, for immoral conduct will then be prohibited by law not just to punish sin or to "force men to be moral," but rather to prevent harm to others. If, however, there are forms of immorality that do not necessarily cause harm, "the problem of the enforcement of morality" becomes especially acute.

The central problem cases are those criminal actions generally called "morals offenses." Offenses against morality and decency have long constituted a category of crimes (as distinct from offenses against the person, offenses against property, and so on). These have included mainly sex offenses, such as adultery, fornication, sodomy, incest, and prostitution, but also a miscellany of nonsexual offenses, including cruelty to animals, desecration of the flag or other venerated symbols, and mistreatment of corpses. In a useful article,[1] Louis B. Schwartz maintains that what sets these crimes off as a class is not their special relation to morality (murder is also an offense against morality, but it is not a "morals offense") but the lack of an essential connection between them and social harm. In particular, their suppression is not required by the public security. Some morals offenses may harm the perpetrators themselves, but the risk of harm of this sort has usually been consented to in advance by the actors. Offense to other parties, when it occurs, is usually a consequence of perpetration of the offenses *in public,* and can be prevented by statutes against "open lewdness," or "solicitation" in public places. That still leaves "morals offenses" committed by consenting adults in private. Should they really be crimes?

In addition to the general presumption against coercion, other arguments against legislation prohibiting private and harmless sexual practices are drawn from the harm principle itself; laws governing private affairs are extremely awkward and expensive to enforce, and have side effects that are invariably harmful. Laws against homosexuality, for example, can only be occasionally and randomly enforced, and this leads to the inequities of selective enforcement and opportunities for blackmail and private vengeance. Moreover, "the pursuit of homosexuals involves policemen in degrading entrapment practices, and diverts attention and effort"[2] from more serious (harmful) crimes of aggression, fraud, and corruption.

These considerations have led some to argue against statutes that prohibit private immorality, but, not surprisingly, it has encouraged others to abandon their exclusive reliance on the harm and/or offense principles, at least in the case of morals offenses. The alternative principle of "legal moralism" has several forms. In its more moderate version it is commonly associated with the views of Patrick Devlin,[3] whose theory, as I understand it, is really an application of the public harm principle. The proper aim of criminal law, he agrees, is the prevention of harm, not merely to individuals, but also (and primarily) to society itself. A shared moral code, Devlin argues, is a necessary condition for the very existence of a community. Shared moral convictions function as "invisible bonds" tying individuals together into an orderly society. Moreover, the fundamental unifying morality (to switch the metaphor) is a kind of "seamless web";[4] to damage it

---

[1] Louis B. Schwartz, "Morals Offenses and the Model Penal Code," *Columbia Law Review,* LXIII (1963), 669 ff.

[2] Schwartz, "Morals Offenses and the Model Penal Code," 671.

[3] Patrick Devlin, *The Enforcement of Morals* (London: Oxford University Press, 1965).

[4] The phrase is not Devlin's but that of his critic, H.L.A. Hart, in *Law, Liberty, and Morality* (Stanford: Stanford University Press, 1963), p. 51. In his rejoinder to Hart, Devlin writes: "Seamlessness presses the simile rather hard but apart from that, I should say that for most people morality is a web of beliefs rather than a number of unconnected ones." Devlin, *The Enforcement of Morals,* p. 115.

at one point is to weaken it throughout. Hence, society has as much right to protect its moral code by legal coercion as it does to protect its equally indispensable political institutions. The law cannot tolerate politically revolutionary activity, nor can it accept activity that rips assunder its moral fabric. "The suppression of vice is as much the law's business as the suppression of subversive activities; it is no more possible to define a sphere of private morality than it is to define one of private subversive activity."[5]

H.L.A. Hart finds it plausible that some shared morality is necessary to the existence of a community, but criticizes Devlin's further contention "that a society is identical with its morality as that is at any given moment of its history, so that a change in its morality is tantamount to the destruction of a society."[6] Indeed, a moral critic might admit that we can't exist as a society without some morality, while insisting that we can perfectly well exist without *this* morality (if we put a better one in its place). Devlin seems to reply that the shared morality *can* be changed even though protected by law, and, when it does change, the emergent reformed morality in turn deserves *its* legal protection.[7] The law then functions to make moral reform difficult, but there is no preventing change where reforming zeal is fierce enough. How does one bring about a change in prevailing moral beliefs when they are enshrined in law? Presumably by advocating conduct which is in fact illegal, by putting into public practice what one preaches, and by demonstrating one's sincerity by marching proudly off to jail for one's convictions:

there is...a natural respect for opinions that are sincerely held. When such opinions accumulate enough weight, the law must either yield or it is broken. In a democratic society...there will be a strong tendency for it to yield—not to abandon all defenses so as to let in the horde, but to give ground to those who are prepared to fight for something that they prize. To fight may be to suffer. A willingness to suffer is the most convincing proof of sincerity. Without the law there would be no proof. The law is the anvil on which the hammer strikes.[8]

In this remarkable passage, Devlin has discovered another argument for enforcing "morality as such," and incidentally for principled civil disobedience as the main technique for initiating and regulating moral change. A similar argument, deriving from Samuel Johnson and applying mainly to changes in religious doctrine, was well known to Mill. According to this theory, religious innovators deserve to be persecuted, for persecution allows them to prove their mettle and demonstrate their disinterested good faith, while their teachings, insofar as they are true, cannot be hurt, since truth will always triumph in the end. Mill held this method of testing

[5] Devlin, *The Enforcement of Morality*, pp. 13–14.
[6] Hart, *Law, Liberty, and Morality*, p. 51.
[7] Devlin, *The Enforcement of Morality*, pp. 115 ff.
[8] Devlin, *The Enforcement of Morality*, p. 116.

truth, whether in science, religion, or morality, to be both uneconomical and ungenerous.[9] But if self-sacrificing civil disobedience is *not* the most efficient and humane remedy for the moral reformer, what instruments of moral change are available to him? This question is not only difficult to answer in its own right, it is also the rock that sinks Devlin's favorite analogy between "harmless" immorality and political subversion.

Consider the nature of subversion. Most modern law-governed countries have a constitution, a set of duly constituted authorities, and a body of statutes created and enforced by these authorities. The ways of changing these things will be well known, orderly, and permitted by the constitution. For example, constitutions are amended, legislators are elected, and new legislation is introduced. On the other hand, it is easy to conceive of various sorts of unpermitted and disorderly change—through assassination and violent revolution, or bribery and subornation, or the use of legitimately won power to extort and intimidate. Only these illegitimate methods of change can be called "subversion." But here the analogy between positive law and positive morality begins to break down. There is no "moral constitution," no well-known and orderly way of introducing moral legislation to duly constituted moral legislators, no clear convention of majority rule. Moral subversion, if there is such a thing, must consist in the employment of disallowed techniques of change instead of the officially permitted "constitutional" ones. It consists not simply of change as such, but of illegitimate change. Insofar as the notion of legitimately induced moral change remains obscure, illegitimate moral change is no better. Still, there is enough content to both notions to preserve some analogy to the political case. A citizen works *legitimately* to change public moral beliefs when he openly and forthrightly expresses his own dissent, when he attempts to argue, persuade, and offer reasons, and when he lives according to his own convictions with persuasive quiet and dignity, neither harming others nor offering counterpersuasive offense to tender sensibilities. A citizen attempts to change mores by *illegitimate* means when he abandons argument and example for force and fraud. If this is the basis of the distinction between legitimate and illegitimate techniques of moral change, then the use of state power to affect moral belief *one way or the other,* when harmfulness is not involved, is a clear example of illegitimacy. Government enforcement of the conventional code is not to be called "moral subversion," of course, because it is used on behalf of the status quo; but whether conservative or innovative, it is equally in defiance of our "moral constitution" (if anything is).

The second version of legal moralism is the pure version, not some other principle in disguise. Enforcement of morality as such and the attendant punishment of sin are not justified as means to some further social aim

---

[9] John Stuart Mill, *On Liberty* (New York: Liberal Arts Press, 1956) pp. 33–34.

(such as preservation of social cohesiveness) but are ends in themselves. Perhaps J. F. Stephen was expressing this pure moralism when he wrote that "there are acts of wickedness so gross and outrageous that...[protection of others apart], they must be prevented at any cost to the offender and punished if they occur with exemplary severity."[10] From his examples it is clear that Stephen had in mind the very acts that are called "morals offenses" in the law.

It is sometimes said in support of pure legal moralism that the world as a whole would be a better place without morally ugly, even "harmlessly immoral," conduct, and that our actual universe is intrinsically worse for having such conduct in it. The threat of punishment, the argument continues, deters such conduct. Actual instances of punishment not only back up the threat, and thus help keep future moral weeds out of the universe's garden, they also erase past evils from the universe's temporal record by "nullifying" them, or making it as if they never were. Thus punishment, it is said, contributes to the intrinsic value of the universe in two ways: by canceling out past sins and preventing future ones.[11]

There is some plausibility in this view when it is applied to ordinary harmful crimes, especially those involving duplicity or cruelty, which really do seem to "set the universe out of joint." It is natural enough to think of repentance, apology, or forgiveness as "setting things straight," and of punishment as a kind of "payment" or a wiping clean of the moral slate. But in cases where it is natural to resort to such analogies, there is not only a rule infraction, there is also a *victim*—some person or society of persons who have been harmed. Where there is no victim—and especially where there is no profit at the expense of another—"setting things straight" has no clear intuitive content.

Punishment may yet play its role in discouraging harmless private immoralities for the sake of "the universe's moral record." But if fear of punishment is to keep people from illicit intercourse (or from desecrating flags, or mistreating corpses) in the privacy of their own rooms, then morality shall have to be enforced with a fearsome efficiency that shows no respect for individual privacy. If private immoralities are to be deterred by threat of punishment, the detecting authorities must be able to look into the hidden chambers and locked rooms of anyone's private domicile. When we put this massive forfeiture of privacy into the balance along with the usual costs of coercion—loss of spontaneity, stunting of rational powers, anxiety, hypocrisy, and the rest—the price of securing mere outward conformity to the community's moral standards (for that is all that can be achieved by the penal law) is exorbitant.

---

[10] James Fitzjames Stephen, *Liberty, Equality, Fraternity* (London: 1873), p. 163.
[11] Cf. C. D. Broad, "Certain Features in Moore's Ethical Doctrines," in P. A. Schilpp, *The Philosophy of G. E. Moore* (Evanston, Ill.: Northwestern University Press, 1942), pp. 48 ff.

Perhaps the most interesting of the nonsexual morals offenses, and the most challenging case for application of liberty-limiting principles, is cruelty to animals. Suppose that John Doe is an intelligent, sensitive person with one very severe neurotic trait—he loves to see living things suffer pain. Fortunately, he never has occasion to torture human beings (he would genuinely regret that), for he can always find an animal for the purpose. For a period he locks himself in his room every night, draws the blind, and then beats and tortures a dog to death. The sounds of shrieks and moans, which are music to his ears, are nuisances to his neighbors, and when his landlady discovers what he has been doing she is so shocked she has to be hospitalized. Distressed that he has caused harm to human beings, Doe leaves the rooming house, buys a five hundred acre ranch, and moves into a house in the remote, unpopulated center of his own property. There, in the perfect privacy of his own home, he spends every evening maiming, torturing, and beating to death his own animals.

What are we to say of Doe's bizarre behavior? We have three alternatives. First we can say that it is perfectly permissible since it consists simply in a man's destruction of his own property. How a man disposes in private of his own property is no concern of anyone else providing he causes no nuisance such as loud noises and evil smells. Second, we can say that this behavior is patently immoral even though it causes no harm to the interests of anyone other than the actor; further, since it obviously should *not* be permitted by the law, this is a case where the harm principle is inadequate and must be supplemented by legal moralism. Third, we can extend the harm principle to animals, and argue that the law can interfere with the private enjoyment of property not to enforce "morality as such," but rather to prevent harm to the animals. The third alternative is the most inviting, but not without its difficulties. We *must* control animal movements, exploit animal labor, and, in many cases, deliberately slaughter animals. All these forms of treatment would be "harm" if inflicted on human beings, but cannot be allowed to count as harm to animals if the harm principle is to be extended to them in a realistic way. The best compromise is to recognize one supreme interest of animals, namely the interest in freedom from cruelly or wantonly inflicted pain, and to count as "harm" all and only invasions of *that* interest.

2. OBSCENITY AND THE OFFENSE PRINCIPLE   Up to this point we have considered the harm and offense principles together in order to determine whether between them they are sufficient to regulate conventional immoralities, or whether they need help from a further independent principle, legal moralism. Morals offenses were treated as essentially private so that the offense principle could not be stretched to apply to them. Obscene literature and pornographic displays would appear to be quite different in this respect. Both are materials deliberately published for the eyes of others, and their existence can bring partisans of the unsupplemented harm principle into direct conflict with those who endorse *both* the harm and offense principles.

In its untechnical, prelegal sense, the word "obscenity" refers to material dealing with nudity, sex, or excretion in an offensive manner. Such material becomes obscene in the legal sense when, because of its offensiveness or for some other reason [this question had best be left open in the definition], it is or ought to be without legal protection. The legal definition then incorporates the everyday sense, and essential to both is the requirement that the material be *offensive*. An item may offend one person and not another. "Obscenity," if it is to avoid this subjective relativity, must involve an interpersonal objective sense of "offensive." Material must be offensive by prevailing community standards that are public and well known, or be such that it is apt to offend virtually everyone.

Not all material that is generally offensive need also be harmful in any sense recognized by the harm principle. It is partly an empirical question whether reading or witnessing obscene material causes social harm; reliable evidence, even of a statistical kind, of causal connections between obscenity and antisocial behavior is extremely hard to find.[12] In the absence of clear and decisive evidence of harmfulness, the American Civil Liberties Union insists that the offensiveness of obscene material cannot be a sufficient ground for its repression:

...the question in a case involving obscenity, just as in every case involving an attempted restriction upon free speech, is whether the words or pictures are used in such circumstances and are of such a nature as to create a clear and present danger that they will bring about a substantial evil that the state has a right to prevent.... We believe that under the current state of knowledge, there is grossly insufficient evidence to show that obscenity brings about *any* substantive evil.[13]

The A.C.L.U. argument employs *only* the harm principle among liberty-limiting principles, and treats literature, drama, and painting as forms of expression subject to the same rules as expressions of opinion. In respect to both types of expression, "every act of deciding what should be barred carries with it a danger to the community."[14] The suppression itself is an evil to the author who is squelched. The power to censor and punish involves risks that socially valuable material will be repressed along with the "filth." The overall effect of suppression, the A.C.L.U. concludes, is

12 There have been some studies made, but the results have been inconclusive. See the *Report of the Federal Commission on Obscenity and Pornography* (New York: Bantam Books, 1970), pp. 169–308.
13 *Obscenity and Censorship* (Pamphlet published by the American Civil Liberties Union, New York, March, 1963), p. 7.
14 *Obscenity and Censorship*, p. 4.

almost certainly to discourage nonconformist and eccentric expression generally. In order to override these serious risks, there must be in a given case an even more clear and present danger that the obscene material, if not squelched, will cause even greater harm; such countervailing evidence is never forthcoming. (If such evidence were to accumulate, the A.C.L.U. would be perfectly willing to change its position on obscenity.)

The A.C.L.U. stand on obscenity seems clearly to be the position dictated by the unsupplemented harm principle and its corollary, the clear and present danger test. Is there any reason at this point to introduce the offense principle into the discussion? Unhappily, we may be forced to if we are to do justice to all of our particular intuitions in the most harmonious way. Consider an example suggested by Professor Schwartz. By the provisions of the new Model Penal Code, he writes, "a rich homosexual may not use a billboard on Times Square to promulgate to the general populace the techniques and pleasures of sodomy."[15] If the notion of "harm" is restricted to its narrow sense, that is, contrasted with "offense," it will be hard to reconstruct a rationale for this prohibition based on the harm principle. There is unlikely to be evidence that a lurid and obscene public poster in Times Square would create a clear and present danger of injury to those who fail to avert their eyes in time as they come blinking out of the subway stations. Yet it will be surpassingly difficult for even the most dedicated liberal to advocate freedom of expression in a case of this kind. Hence, if we are to justify coercion in this case, we will likely be driven, however reluctantly, to the offense principle.

There is good reason to be "reluctant" to embrace the offense principle until driven to it by an example like the above. People take perfectly genuine offense at many socially useful or harmless activities, from commercial advertisements to inane chatter. Moreover, widespread irrational prejudices can lead people to be disgusted, shocked, even morally repelled by perfectly innocent activities, and we should be loath to permit their groundless repugnance to override the innocence. The offense principle, therefore, must be formulated very precisely and applied in accordance with carefully formulated standards so as not to open the door to wholesale and intuitively unwarranted repression. At the very least we should require that the prohibited conduct or material be of the sort apt to offend almost everybody, and not just some shifting majority or special interest group.

It is instructive to note that a strictly drawn offense principle would not only justify prohibition of conduct and pictured conduct that is in its inherent character repellent, but also conduct and pictured conduct that is inoffensive in itself but offensive in inappropriate circumstances. I have in mind so-called indecencies such as public nudity. One can imagine an

15 Schwartz, "Morals Offenses and the Penal Code," 680.

advocate of the unsupplemented harm principle arguing against the public nudity prohibition on the grounds that the sight of a naked body does no one any harm, and the state has no right to impose standards of dress or undress on private citizens. How one chooses to dress, after all, is a form of self-expression. If we do not permit the state to bar clashing colors or bizarre hair styles, by what right does it prohibit total undress? Perhaps the sight of naked people could at first lead to riots or other forms of antisocial behavior, but that is precisely the sort of contingency for which we have police. If we don't take away a person's right of free speech for the reason that its exercise may lead others to misbehave, we cannot in consistency deny his right to dress or undress as he chooses for the same reason.

There may be no answering this challenge on its own ground, but the offense principle provides a ready rationale for the nudity prohibition. The sight of nude bodies in public places is for almost everyone acutely *embarrassing*. Part of the explanation no doubt rests on the fact that nudity has an irresistible power to draw the eye and focus the thoughts on matters that are normally repressed. The conflict between these attracting and repressing forces is exciting, upsetting, and anxiety-producing. In some persons it will create at best a kind of painful turmoil, and at worst that experience of exposure to oneself of "peculiarly sensitive, intimate, vulnerable aspects of the self"[16] which is called *shame*. "One's feeling is involuntarily exposed openly in one's face; one is uncovered...taken by surprise...made a fool of."[17] The result is not mere "offense," but a kind of psychic jolt that in many normal people can be a painful wound. Even those of us who are better able to control our feelings might well resent the *nuisance* of having to do so.

If we are to accept the offense principle as a supplement to the harm principle, we must accept two corollaries which stand in relation to it similarly to the way in which the clear and present danger test stands to the harm principle. The first, the *standard of universality,* has already been touched upon. For the offensiveness (disgust, embarrassment, outraged sensibilities, or shame) to be sufficient to warrant coercion, it should be the reaction that could be expected from almost any person chosen at random from the nation as a whole, regardless of sect, faction, race, age, or sex. The second is the *standard of reasonable avoidability.* No one has a right to protection from the state against offensive experiences if he can effectively avoid those experiences with no unreasonable effort or inconvenience. If a nude person enters a public bus and takes a seat near the front, there may be no effective way for other patrons to avoid intensely shameful embarrassment (or other insupportable feelings) short of leaving

---

[16] Helen Merrill Lynd, *On Shame and the Search for Identity* (New York: Science Editions, Inc., 1961), p. 33.

[17] Lynd, *On Shame and the Search for Identity,* p. 32.

the bus, which would be an unreasonable inconvenience. Similarly, obscene remarks over a loudspeaker, homosexual billboards in Times Square, and pornographic handbills thrust into the hands of passing pedestrians all fail to be reasonably avoidable.

On the other hand, the offense principle, properly qualified, can give no warrant to the suppression of *books* on the grounds of obscenity. When printed words hide decorously behind covers of books sitting passively on bookstore shelves, their offensiveness is easily avoided. The contrary view is no doubt encouraged by the common comparison of obscenity with "smut," "filth," or "dirt." This in turn suggests an analogy to nuisance law, which governs cases where certain activities create loud noises or terrible odors offensive to neighbors, and "the courts must weigh the gravity of the nuisance [substitute "offense"] to the neighbors against the social utility [substitute "redeeming social value"] of the defendant's conduct."[18] There is, however, one vitiating disanalogy in this comparison. In the case of "dirty books" the offense is easily avoidable. There is nothing like the evil smell of rancid garbage oozing right out through the covers of a book. When an "obscene" book sits on a shelf, who is there to be offended? Those who want to read it for the sake of erotic stimulation presumably will not be offended (or else they wouldn't read it), and those who choose not to read it will have no experience by which to be offended. If its covers are too decorous, some innocents may browse through it by mistake and be offended by what they find, but they need only close the book to escape the offense. Even this offense, minimal as it is, could be completely avoided by prior consultation of trusted book reviewers. I conclude that there are no sufficient grounds derived either from the harm or offense principles for suppressing obscene literature, unless that ground be the protection of children; but I can think of no reason why restrictions on sales to children cannot work as well for printed materials as they do for cigarettes and whiskey.

3. LEGAL PATERNALISM*

The liberty-limiting principle called legal paternalism justifies state coercion to protect individuals from self-inflicted harm, or, in its extreme version, to guide them, whether they like it or not, toward their own good. Parents can be expected to justify interference in the lives of their children (e.g., telling them what they must eat and when they must sleep) on the ground that "daddy knows best." Legal paternalism seems to imply that, since the state

---

[18] William L. Prosser, *Handbook of the Law of Torts* (St. Paul: West Publishing Co., 1955), p. 411.

* This section reprinted from my "Legal Paternalism" in Volume I, no. 1 of the *Canadian Journal of Philosophy* (1971), by permission of the Canadian Association for Publishing in Philosophy.

often perceives the interests of individual citizens better than do the citizens themselves, it stands as a permanent guardian of those interests *in loco parentis.* Put this bluntly, paternalism seems a preposterous doctrine. If adults are treated as children they will come in time to be like children. Deprived of the right to choose for themselves, they will soon lose the power of rational judgment and decision. Even children, after a certain point, had better not be "treated as children," or they will never acquire the outlook and capability of responsible adults.

Yet if we reject paternalism entirely, and deny that a person's own good is ever a valid ground for coercing him, we seem to fly in the face both of common sense and long-established customs and laws. In the criminal law, for example, a prospective victim's freely granted consent is no defense to the charge of mayhem or homicide. The state simply refuses to permit anyone to agree to his own disablement or killing. The law of contracts similarly refuses to recognize as valid contracts to sell oneself into slavery, or to become a mistress, or a second wife. Any ordinary citizen is legally justified in using reasonable force to prevent another from mutilating himself or committing suicide. No one is allowed to purchase certain drugs even for therapeutic purposes without a physician's prescription (doctor knows best). The use of other drugs, such as heroin, for mere pleasure is not permitted under any circumstances. It is hard to find any convincing rationale for all such restrictions apart from the argument that beatings, mutilations, death, concubinage, slavery, and bigamy are always bad for a person whether he or she knows it or not, and that antibiotics are too dangerous for any nonexpert, and narcotics for anyone at all, to take on his own initiative.

The trick is stopping short once one undertakes this path, unless we wish to ban whiskey, cigarettes, and fried foods, which tend to be bad for people, too. We must somehow reconcile our general repugnance for paternalism with the apparent necessity, or at least reasonableness, of some paternalistic regulations. The way to do this is to find mediating maxims or standards of application for the paternalistic principle which restrict its use in a way analogous to that in which the universality and reasonable avoidance tests delimit the offense principle. Let us begin by rejecting the views that the protection of a person from himself is *always* a valid ground for interference and that it is *never* a valid ground. It follows that it is a valid ground only under certain conditions, which we must now try to state.

It will be useful to make some preliminary distinctions. The first is between those cases in which a person directly produces harm to himself (where the harm is the certain and desired end of his conduct), and those cases in which a person simply creates a *risk* of harm to himself in the course of activities directed toward other ends. The man who knowingly swallows a lethal dose of arsenic will certainly die, and death must be imputed as his goal. Another man is offended by the sight of his left hand, so he grasps an ax in his right hand and chops his left hand off. He does not thereby "endanger" his interest in the physical integrity of his limbs, or "risk" the loss of his hand; he brings about the loss directly and deliberately. On the other hand, to smoke cigarettes or to drive at excessive speeds is not to harm oneself directly, but rather to increase beyond a normal level the probability that harm to oneself will result.

The second distinction is that between reasonable and unreasonable risks. There is no form of activity (or inactivity, for that matter) that does not involve some risks. On some occasions we have a choice between more and less risky actions, and prudence dictates that we take the less risky course. However, what is called "prudence" is not always reasonable. Sometimes it is more reasonable to assume a great risk for a great gain than to play it safe and forfeit a unique opportunity. Thus, it is not necessarily more reasonable for a coronary patient to increase his life expectancy by living a life of quiet inactivity than to continue working hard at his career in the hope of achieving something important, even at the risk of a sudden fatal heart attack. Although there is no simple mathematical formula to guide one in making such decisions or for judging them "reasonable" or "unreasonable," there are some decisions that are manifestly unreasonable. It is unreasonable to drive at sixty miles an hour through a twenty mile an hour zone in order to arrive at a party on time, but it may be reasonable to drive fifty miles an hour to get a pregnant wife to the maternity ward. It is foolish to resist an armed robber in an effort to protect one's wallet, but it may be worth a desperate lunge to protect one's very life.

All of these cases involve a number of distinct considerations. If there is time to deliberate one should consider: (1) the degree of probability that harm to oneself will result from a given course of action, (2) the seriousness of the harm being risked, i.e., "the value or importance of that which is exposed to the risk," (3) the degree of probability that the goal inclining one to shoulder the risk will in fact result from the course of action, (4) the value or importance of achieving that goal, that is, just how worthwhile it is to one (this is the intimately personal factor, requiring a decision about one's own preferences, that makes it so difficult for the outsider to judge the reasonableness of a risk), and (5) the necessity of the risk, that is, the availability or absence of alternative, less risky, means to the desired goal.[19]

Certain judgments about the reasonableness of risk assumptions are quite uncontroversial. We can say, for example, that the greater are considerations 1 and 2, the less reasonable the risk, and the greater are considerations 3, 4, and 5, the more reasonable the risk. But in a given difficult case, even where questions of "probability" are meaningful and beyond dispute, and where all the relevant facts are known, the risk decision may defy objective

---

[19] The distinctions in this paragraph have been borrowed from Henry T. Terry, "Negligence," *Harvard Law Review*, XXIX (1915), pp. 40–50.

assessment because of its component personal value judgments. In any case, if the state is to be given the right to prevent a person from risking harm to himself (and only himself), it must not be on the ground that the prohibited action is risky, or even extremely risky, but rather that the risk is extreme and, in respect to its objectively assessable components, manifestly unreasonable. There are sometimes very good reasons for regarding even a person's judgment of personal worthwhileness (consideration 4) to be "manifestly unreasonable," but it remains to be seen whether (or when) that kind of unreasonableness can be sufficient grounds for interference.

The third and final distinction is between fully voluntary and not fully voluntary assumptions of a risk. One assumes a risk in a fully voluntary way when one shoulders it while informed of all relevant facts and contingencies, and in the absence of all coercive pressure or compulsion. To whatever extent there is neurotic compulsion, misinformation, excitement or impetuousness, clouded judgment (as, e.g., from alcohol), or immature or defective faculties of reasoning, the choice falls short of perfect voluntariness.[20] Voluntariness, then, is a matter of degree. One's "choice" is *completely involuntary* when it is no choice at all, properly speaking—when one lacks all muscular control of one's movements, or is knocked down or sent reeling by a blow or an explosion—or when, through ignorance, one chooses something other than what one means to choose, as when one thinks the arsenic powder is table salt and sprinkles it on one's scrambled eggs. Most harmful choices, as most choices generally, fall somewhere between the extremes of perfect voluntariness and complete involuntariness.

The central thesis of Mill and other individualists about paternalism is that the fully voluntary choice or consent (to another's doing) of a mature and rational human being concerning matters that directly affect only his own interests is so precious that no one else (especially the state) has a right to interfere with it simply for the person's "own good." No doubt this thesis was also meant to apply to almost-but-not-quite fully voluntary choices as well, and probably even to some substantially nonvoluntary ones (e.g., a neurotic person's choice of a wife who will satisfy his neurotic needs, but only at the price of great unhappiness, eventual divorce, and exacerbated guilt). However, it is not probable that the individualist thesis was meant to apply to choices near the bottom of the voluntariness scale, and Mill himself left no doubt that he did not intend it to apply to completely involuntary "choices." Neither should we expect antipaternalistic individualism to deny protection to a person from his own nonvoluntary choices, for insofar as the choices are not voluntary they are just as alien to him as the choices of someone else.

[20] My usage of the term "voluntary" differs from that of Aristotle in his famous analysis in Book III of the *Nicomachean Ethics,* but corresponds closely to what Aristotle called "deliberate choice."

Thus Mill would permit the state to protect a man from his own ignorance, at least in circumstances that create a strong presumption that his uninformed or misinformed choice would not correspond to his eventual enlightened one.

If either a public officer or anyone else saw a person attempting to cross a bridge which had been ascertained to be unsafe, and there were no time to warn him of his danger, they might seize him and turn him back, without any real infringement of his liberty; for liberty consists in doing what one desires, and he does not desire to fall into the river.[21]

Of course, for all the public officer may know, the man on the bridge does desire to fall into the river, or to take the risk of falling for other purposes. Then, Mill argues, if the person is fully warned of the danger and wishes to proceed anyway, that is his business alone, despite the advance presumption that most people do not wish to run such risks. Hence the officer was justified, Mill would argue, in his original interference.

On other occasions a person may need to be protected from some other condition that may render his informed choice substantially less than voluntary. He may be "a child, or delirious, or in some state of excitement or absorption incompatible with the full use of the reflecting faculty."[22] Mill would not permit any such person to cross an objectively unsafe bridge. On the other hand, there is no reason why a child, or an excited person, or a drunkard, or a mentally ill person should not be allowed to proceed on his way home across a perfectly safe thoroughfare. Even substantially non-voluntary choices deserve protection unless there is good reason to judge them dangerous.

For all we can know, the behavior of a drunk or an emotionally upset person would be exactly the same even if he were sober and calm. But when the behavior seems patently self-damaging and is of a sort in which most calm and normal persons would not engage, then there are strong grounds, if only of a statistical sort, for inferring the opposite; these grounds, on Mill's principle, would justify interference. It may be that there is no kind of action of which it can be said, "No mentally competent adult in a calm, attentive mood, fully informed, and so on, would ever choose (or consent to) that." Nevertheless, there are some actions that create a powerful presumption that an actor in his right mind would not choose them. The point of calling this hypothesis a "presumption" is to require that it be completely overridden before legal permission be given to a person who has already been interfered with to go on as before. For example, if a policeman (or anyone else) sees John Doe about to chop off his hand with an ax, he is perfectly justified in using force to prevent him, because of the presumption that no one could voluntarily choose to do such a thing. The presumption, however, should always be taken as rebuttable in

21 Mill, *On Liberty*, p. 117.
22 Mill, *On Liberty*, p. 117.

principle; it will be up to Doe to prove before an official tribunal that he is calm, competent, and free, and still wishes to chop off his hand. Perhaps this is too great a burden to expect Doe himself to "prove," but the tribunal should require that the presumption against voluntariness be overturned by evidence from some source or other. The existence of the presumption should require that an objective determination be made, whether by the usual adversary procedures of law courts, or simply by a collective investigation by the tribunal into the available facts. The greater the presumption to be overridden, the more elaborate and fastidious should be the legal paraphernalia required, and the stricter the standards of evidence. The point of the procedure would not be to evaluate the wisdom or worthiness of a person's choice, but rather to determine whether the choice really is his.

This seems to lead us to a form of paternalism so weak and innocuous that it could be accepted even by Mill, namely, that the state has the right to prevent self-regarding harmful conduct only when it is substantially nonvoluntary, or when temporary intervention is necessary to establish whether it is voluntary or not. A strong presumption that no normal person would voluntarily choose or consent to the kind of conduct in question should be a proper ground for detaining the person until the voluntary character of his choice can be established. We can use the phrase "the standard of voluntariness" as a label for considerations that mediate application of the principle that a person can be protected from his own folly.

Consider a typical hard case for the application of the voluntariness standard, the problem of harmful drugs. Suppose that Richard Roe requests a prescription of drug X from Dr. Doe, and the following discussion ensues:

DR. DOE: I cannot prescribe drug X to you because it will do you physical harm.
MR. ROE: But you are mistaken. It will not cause me physical harm.

In a case like this, the state, of course, backs the doctor, since it deems medical questions to be technical matters subject to expert opinions. If a layman disagrees with a physician on a question of medical fact, the layman is presumed wrong, and if he nevertheless chooses to act on his factually mistaken belief, his action will be substantially less than fully voluntary. That is, the action of *ingesting a substance which will in fact harm him* is not the action he voluntarily chooses to do (because he does not believe that it is harmful). Hence the state intervenes to protect him not from his own free and voluntary choices, but from his own ignorance.

Suppose however that the exchange goes as follows:

DR. DOE: I cannot prescribe drug X to you because it will do you physical harm.
MR. ROE: Exactly. That's just what I want. I want to harm myself.

In this case Roe is properly apprised of the facts; he suffers from no delusions or misconceptions. Yet his choice is so odd that there exists a reasonable presumption that he has been deprived of the "full use of his reflecting faculty." It is because we know that the overwhelming majority of choices to inflict injury for its own sake on oneself are not fully voluntary that we are entitled to presume that the present choice is not fully voluntary. If no further evidence of derangement, illness, severe depression, or unsettling excitation can be discovered, however, and the patient can convince an objective panel that his choice is voluntary (unlikely event!), then our "voluntariness standard" would permit no further state constraint.

Now consider the third possibility:

DR. DOE: I cannot prescribe drug X to you because it is very likely to do you physical harm.

MR. ROE: I don't care if it causes me physical harm. I'll get a lot of pleasure first, so much pleasure, in fact, that it is well worth running the risk of physical harm. If I must pay a price for my pleasure I am willing to do so.

This is perhaps the most troublesome case. Roe's choice is not patently irrational on its face. A well thought-out philosophical hedonism may be one of his profoundest convictions, involving a fundamental decision of principle to commit himself to the intensely pleasurable, even if brief, life. If no third party interests are directly involved, the state can hardly be permitted to declare his philosophical convictions unsound or "sick" and prevent him from practicing them, without assuming powers that it will inevitably misuse.

On the other hand, this case may be quite similar to the preceding one, depending on what the exact facts are. If the drug is known to give only an hour's mild euphoria and then cause an immediate, violently painful death, then the risks appear so unreasonable as to create a powerful presumption of nonvoluntariness. The desire to commit suicide must always be presumed to be both nonvoluntary and harmful to others until shown otherwise. (Of course, in some cases it can be shown otherwise.) Alternatively, drug X may be harmful in the way nicotine is now known to be harmful; twenty or thirty years of heavy use may create a grave risk of lung cancer or heart disease. Using the drug for pleasure when the risks are of this kind may be to run unreasonable risks, but that is no strong evidence of nonvoluntariness. Many perfectly normal, rational persons voluntarily choose to run precisely these risks for whatever pleasures they find in smoking. To assure itself that such practices are truly voluntary, the state should continually confront smokers with the ugly medical facts so that there is no escaping the knowledge of the exact medical risks to health. Constant reminders of the hazards should be at every hand, with no softening of the gory details. The state might even be justified in using its taxing, regulatory, and persuasive powers to make smoking (and similar drug usage) more difficult or less attractive; but to prohibit it outright would be to tell the voluntary risk-taker that his informed judgments of what is worthwhile are less reasonable than those of the state, and therefore he may not act on them. This is paternalism of the strong kind, unmediated by the voluntariness standard. As a principle of public policy it has an acrid moral flavor, and creates serious risks of governmental tyranny.

4. COLLECTIVE GOODS AND COLLECTIVE ACTION Despite the presumptive case for liberty, there seem to be numerous examples in which the modern state has no choice but to force (usually by compulsory taxation) both willing and unwilling citizens to support public projects that are clearly in the public interest. In many of these cases those who do not benefit directly from a public service are made to pay as much in its support as those who do, or even more. Thus nondrivers are taxed to support highways and nonparents to support schools. This has the appearance of injustice, and the justification of unhappy necessity. Often the alternative to mandatory taxation—a system of purely voluntary support requiring only users to pay fees—is subject to a fatal defect that forces us to choose between universal compulsory support for the public facility or no facility at all.

Consider, for example, public municipal parks. Suppose the town of Metropolis decides to create a large public park with gardens, woods, trails, and playgrounds. John Doe appreciates living in an attractive community but has no direct personal need for such a park, since he already has a ten acre yard with gardens, picnic tables, tennis courts, and the like. Why, he asks, should he be forced to support something he doesn't need and doesn't want strongly enough to pay for? Suppose, however, that the city charges only those who wish to use the park, and that this group constitutes 90 percent of the population. The richest 10 percent opt out, thus raising the average costs to the remainder. That rise, in turn, forces some of the 90 percent to withdraw, thus raising the cost to the others, forcing still more to drop out, and so on. This process will continue until either a very expensive equilibrium is reached, or, what is more likely, the whole project collapses (as in the case of some voluntary public medical and insurance plans).

It is avoidance of this characteristic escalation effect, rather than paternalism, that provides the rationale for compulsory social security and medicare programs. Here it is important to apply the various principles of liberty distribution not to individual cases, such as the compulsory taxation of John Doe, but to rules and general financing schemes. Compulsory rather than voluntary schemes are justified when the social good in question cannot be secured in any other way. Whether compulsion on this ground accords with the harm principle depends on whether loss of the good would be classified as a social harm or the mere withholding of a benefit (see pp. 29–31). Where the good is security, medical care, or education, there is little doubt that its loss would properly be called a "harm" to those who incur it.

In cases of the sort we have been considering, some people who don't want a given public service are forced to pay for it because there is no other practical way of supporting it, and its loss would be a harm to those who do want it. In a more interesting and troublesome kind of case, *all* of the members of a community or group want some good which is in fact in the interests of each individual equally, and yet it is in no individual's interest to contribute toward the goal unless all are *made* to do so. This paradoxical state of affairs has attracted considerable attention from economists who have noticed its similarity to the condition of a company in an industry that enjoys "perfect competition." So long as the price of a manufactured product on the free market exceeds the marginal cost of production, it will be in the interest of each company to increase its output and thus maximize its profit. But the consequence of increased output will be lower prices, so in the end all companies will be worse off for "maximizing profits" than they might otherwise have been. If any single firm, anticipating this unhappy result, were to restrict its own output unilaterally, it would be in still more trouble, for its restriction of output in a large industry would not prevent the fall of prices, and it would suffer lower sales in addition to lower prices. It is in the interest of each firm that *all the others* restrict output, but, in a purely competitive situation, none of the others dare do that. Where there is no coercion, we have the paradoxical result that it is "rational" for each firm to pursue policies that will destroy its interests in the end. It is more rational still to prefer general coercion.

Problems like that raised by "perfect competition" tend to occur wherever large organizations have come into existence to advance the interests of their members. A great many such organizations, from consumer societies and labor unions to (as many have claimed) the political state itself, exist primarily to advance some common interest in virtue of which the members can be supposed to have banded together in the first place. Now, some of the collective aims to which large organizations are devoted have a very special character. They are directed at goods which, if they are made available to any one member of the group, cannot feasibly be withheld from any other member. Examples of such generalized and indivisible goods are supported prices for companies in the same industry in a not-so-competitive market, the power of collective bargaining for members of a union, and certain goods provided for its citizens by the state, such as police protection, courts of law, armies, navies, and public health agencies. Perhaps it would be technically possible to "sell" these goods only to those willing to pay for them, but it would hardly be "feasible." It is not clear, for example, how an organization, private or public, could eliminate air pollution only for those willing to pay. Nonpayers would breathe the expensively purified air, and there would be no way of preventing this "freeloading" short of banishment or capital punishment. In such cases, it is in each member's interest to let the others pay the bill and then share in consumption of the indivisible benefit; since each member knows that every member knows this as well as he, each has reason to think that he may be taken advantage of if he voluntarily pays his share. Yet if each member, following his own self-interest, refuses to pay, the collective good for which they are united cannot be achieved. Voluntarily submitting to a coercion understood by each to apply to all seems the only way out.

It is in virtue of such considerations that compulsory taxation, at least in support of collective goods and indivisible services of an essential kind, can be justified by the harm principle. That principle would not justify compulsory taxation in support of benefits to private groups, or even of public benefits of the sort whose loss would not constitute a serious harm, but that does not mean that the friends of public libraries, museums, and parks need be driven to embrace the welfare principle (supra, p. 33). When persons and groups are deprived of what they *need*, they are harmed; it may not be implausible to insist that the country as a whole, in this and future generations (including people who have no present desire for culture, history, nature, or beauty), *needs* large national parks, wilderness areas, enormous libraries, museums, atomic accelerators for physical research, huge telescopes, and so on. To argue that we need these things is to claim that we cannot in the end get along very well without them. That is the kind of case that must be made if we are to justify compulsion, on liberal principles, to the reluctant taxpayer.

CHAPTER FOUR

Legal Rights

What is the difference between being *at liberty* to do (omit, have, or be) something and having a *right* to do (etc.) it? In this chapter we shall be concerned with freedom only as viewed from the juridical perspective, with permissibility under rules rather than with the absence of de facto constraints generally. The duties imposed by rules and authorities can themselves function as constraints. Hence, we can with perfect propriety speak of the absence of duty itself as a kind of freedom; but to avoid confusion, we had better say of the person who has no duty to do something that he is *at liberty* not to do that thing, reserving the vocabulary of "freedom" for resultant de facto abilities. Thus, a person might be at liberty to do *X*, and yet not be free to do *X* because he is constrained by something other than duty. The "liberty" to which we refer is conferred by the very systems of rules and regulations that also create rights and duties.

Rights and liberties are bestowed by rules of many different kinds—rules of games such as chess and baseball, rules of nongovernmental institutions such as clubs and learned societies, even the rules of logic, which grant us, under certain conditions, the "right to infer." The concepts of a right and a liberty (as opposed to freedom generally) probably originated however, in systems of juridical law, and it is in legal systems that they have their most subtle and interesting applications and most thorough and detailed elaborations. For that reason it will be instructive to take juridical law as our model, and attempt to understand its relatively definite employment of the concepts that interest us, before turning to the more troublesome uses of those concepts in moral discourse.

1. RIGHTS, LIBERTIES, AND PRIVILEGES

Legal writers[1] commonly distinguish "rights in a strict and narrow sense," usually called *claim-rights,* from "mere liberties," often called *privileges* and sometimes *licenses.* A liberty or privilege in this sense is simply the absence of a duty. To say that Doe is privileged or at liberty to do X is to say that Doe has no duty to refrain from doing X. Normally all citizens are under an obligation to refrain from striking other persons. The criminal law, in forbidding assaults, imposes such a duty on everyone. If Roe nevertheless assaults Doe, then Doe has the legal privilege of striking back in self-defense; he is free of his usual duty of forbearance. Similarly, if Doe is sworn in as a witness, he acquires the liberty of saying words about other persons that it was "previously his legal duty not to say."[2] Sometimes the law leaves two or more persons in a competitive situation in which each person is privileged to do something at the expense of the other. If Doe and Roe each see a fifty dollar bill on the sidewalk, neither has a duty to let the other have it. Rather, both are privileged to get it if they can, though neither is at liberty to use force or violence in the process.

There are several narrower senses of "privilege" in the law in which the word stands not for just *any* liberty but rather a liberty (absence of duty) of some special kind. In one of these senses, a privilege is "a particular and peculiar benefit or advantage enjoyed by a person or group beyond the common advantages of other citizens...an exceptional or extraordinary power or exemption."[3] The word in this sense tends to be pejorative. This kind of exemption is not necessarily justified, and political equalitarians tend to rail against "privilege," so conceived, as simply arbitrary favoritism. Sometimes the suggestion of arbitrariness is nullified by explicit definition, as when the word is defined as "an exemption from some burden or attendance with which certain persons are indulged because the stations they fill or the offices they are engaged in are such as require all their time

[1] The classic source for the analysis of legal relations into rights, liberties, powers, and immunities is Wesley Hohfeld, *Fundamental Legal Conceptions* (New Haven: Yale University Press, 1923). One of the clearest simple expositions of the analysis is that of Arthur L. Corbin, "Legal Analysis and Terminology," *Yale Law Journal,* XXIX (1919), 163–73.

[2] Corbin, "Legal Analysis and Terminology," 165.

[3] *Black's Law Dictionary,* 4th ed. (St. Paul, Minn.: West Publishing Co., 1951), p. 1359.

and care."4 Thus in some jurisdictions physicians are not required to appear in court when they are defendants in malpractice suits, and ambulance drivers everywhere are allowed to exceed speed limits.

The most common of the special legal definitions of a privilege is "a license to invade another's right." If we think of that domain of freedom in which the state protects an individual by imposing duties of noninterference upon all outsiders (the model being a fenced-in area of land with a lock on the gate), then we can think of those who are privileged as persons who are permitted to carry keys to the lock on the gate. Most protective rules are formulated in terms of rights and duties, but exceptions are put in the language of "privilege," so that privileges are "particular and peculiar," the result of special circumstances not included in the rationale of the rule. For example, consent is a form of privilege which allows one to have sexual intercourse without committing rape, or to utter false and damaging remarks without committing slander, or to walk on another's land without committing trespass. Police officers, in virtue of their office, can often lock up persons without committing false imprisonment. These are examples of special possession of a key to invade what would otherwise be another's right. Some more imaginative writers speak of privilege as an area "carved out" of other people's rights. If liberties are to be distinguished from privileges in any of these senses, it is primarily in view of the specially delimited distribution of the latter. The law can leave everyone at liberty in a certain respect, but privileges (in the special senses) necessarily belong either to a particular few or else to everyone in very special circumstances.

There is finally a sense of "privilege" which refers to a kind of legal benefit which is less secure than a right and is often described as a "mere privilege." A driver's license gives a person a right to drive an automobile in the sense that it imposes a duty of noninterference on others that is enforced by the state. This valuable benefit differs from some other rights in that one must make application for it. One must assume the burden of demonstrating to state officials that one is worthy of it; it is granted at the discretion of the state, and is very easily forfeitable. The state, in short, is under no duty to confer the benefit on me. It is nothing I can demand as my due. Rather the state grants or withholds it at its pleasure, and since I have no choice but to take it on the state's own terms, it is a *mere* privilege. A privilege in this sense may be either a liberty (privilege in the earlier sense) or a claim-right in the sense to be explained below. What distinguishes a privilege in this sense is its lack of guarantee. It is the basis of no correlative state duty, and can be withheld or withdrawn by the state at its pleasure.

Rights in the strict sense stand in sharp contrast to both liberties and

4 *Black's Law Dictionary*, p. 1359.

(especially) "mere revocable privileges." Legal claim-rights are necessarily the grounds of other people's duties toward the right-holder. A legal right is a claim to performance, either action or forbearance as the case may be, usually against other private persons. It is also a claim against the state to recognition and enforcement.

What have come to be standard examples of claim-rights were given by Corbin.[5] *B* owes *A* one hundred dollars. That is, *B* has a duty to pay *A* that amount, and that duty seen from *A*'s perspective is *A*'s right to receive one hundred dollars. *B* contracts to deliver goods to *A*, hence *A* has a right to receive those goods from *B*, and that right is simply *B*'s contractual duty seen from *A*'s vantage point. *A* has a right that *B* shall not strike him, and that right (unlike a mere liberty) entails a corresponding duty of *B*'s not to strike *A*.

One can have a liberty which is not also a right, but one cannot have a right which is not also a liberty, for rights can be understood to contain liberties as components. If I have a right to do *X*, then I cannot also have a duty to refrain from doing *X*. But to say that I lack a duty to refrain is to say that I have a liberty or privilege to do. Hence, if I have a right to do *X*, I must also be at liberty to do *X*. What the right adds to the liberty is the duty of others not to interfere.

Legal claim-rights are indispensably valuable possessions. A world without claim-rights, no matter how full of benevolence and devotion to duty, would suffer an immense moral impoverishment. Persons would no longer hope for decent treatment from others on the ground of desert or rightful claim. Indeed, they would come to think of themselves as having no special claim to kindness or consideration from others, so that whenever even minimally decent treatment is forthcoming they would think themselves lucky rather than inherently deserving, and their benefactors extraordinarily virtuous and worthy of great gratitude. The harm to individual self-esteem and character development would be incalculable.[6]

A claim-right, on the other hand, can be urged, pressed, or rightly demanded against other persons. In appropriate circumstances the right-holder can "urgently, peremptorily, or insistently"[7] call for his rights, or assert them authoritatively, confidently, unabashedly. Rights are not mere gifts or favors, motivated by love or pity, for which gratitude is the sole fitting response. A right is something a man can *stand* on, something that can be demanded or insisted upon without embarrassment or shame. When

---

[5] Corbin, "Legal Analysis and Terminology," pp. 164–66.

[6] The effects of this kind of treatment on Southern Negroes is vividly described by Richard Wasserstrom, "Rights, Human Rights and Racial Discrimination," *Journal of Philosophy*, LXI (1964), 628–41.

[7] G. J. Warnock, "Claims to Knowledge," *Proceedings of the Aristotelian Society*, Supplementary volume 36 (1962), p. 21.

that to which one has a right is not forthcoming, the appropriate reaction is indignation; when it is duly given there is no reason for gratitude, since it is simply one's own or one's due that one received. A world with claim-rights is one in which all persons, as actual or potential claimants, are dignified objects of respect, both in their own eyes and in the view of others. No amount of love and compassion, or obedience to higher authority, or noblesse oblige, can substitute for those values.

2. CLASSIFICATION OF CLAIM-RIGHTS

Legal claim-rights can be classified in various ways. If we consider the structures of the rights themselves, that is, their characteristic patterns of involved persons and performances, distinctions can be made between in personam rights and in rem rights, between positive and negative rights, and between active and passive negative rights.

The simplest and earliest model of an in personam right is that of a creditor against his debtor. If Abel owes Baker five dollars, he has a duty to Baker to repay that amount, and Baker can insist that Abel discharge his duty, and can rightly complain if he doesn't. Baker's right holds against one assignable person, Abel. The distinguishing characteristic of in personam rights is that they are correlated with specific duties of determinate individuals. Other examples of such rights are the rights of landlords to collect rent from their tenants, and the rights of the wrongfully injured to damages from their injurers.

In rem rights, on the other hand, are those said to hold not against some specific namable person or persons, but against "the world at large." Examples include a homeowner's right to peaceful occupancy of his own house, a landowner's right to exclusive enjoyment of his land, and anyone's rights to the use or possession of the money in his own purse or pocket. Corresponding to these rights are the legally enforced duties of noninterference imposed on everyone. *Everyone* has a duty to keep off my land without my permission, although in special circumstances specific persons may be privileged to "invade my right," i.e., their duties of noninterference may be temporarily suspended.

The distinction between positive and negative claim-rights is (perhaps deceptively) simple. A *positive* right is a right to other persons' positive actions; a *negative* right is a right to other persons' omissions or fore-bearances. For every positive right I have, someone else has a duty to *do* something; for every negative right I have, someone else has a duty to *refrain* from doing something. Typically, in personam rights are positive and in rem rights are negative. My in personam right against Jones to the repayment of his debt is a right to positive action from him, whereas my in rem right to the contents of my wallet is a claim against everyone to refrain from taking those contents. There are, however, some examples of both negative in personam rights and positive in rem rights. The right of an accident victim to be assisted by anyone who happens to be in a position to help is positive and in rem. It holds against "the whole world" in the same sense as the paradigmatic negative in rem right of a landowner holds against "the whole world." In the latter case, anybody in a position to enter my land has a duty to refrain (unless he has my permission). Negative in personam rights are harder to find. One class of examples involves voluntary forfeiture by a determinate individual of a positive right he shared in common with all others. For example, if you promise me to stay off the public road near my home, then I have a right against you to your forebearance which is in personam because it holds only against a determinate person, and negative because it is correlated with a duty to refrain from acting in a certain way.[8]

Negative rights are, by and large, rights against others not to be interfered with. They can be divided into two important subclasses in a distinction that cuts across that between in personam and in rem negative rights. *Active* rights are rights to act or not act as one chooses; *passive* rights are rights not to be done to by others in certain ways. Among one's active rights may be such as the rights to go where one will and say whatever one pleases, often referred to concisely as "the right to liberty." Among one's passive rights may be such as the rights to be let alone, to enjoy one's property, to keep one's affairs secret, or one's reputation undamaged, or one's body unharmed. These are often characterized collectively as "the right to security." That one person's active rights can be protected only at the expense of another's passive rights, and vice versa, is perhaps the major source of moral perplexity in the political governance of free men. We shall return to the problem of resolving conflicts between liberty and safety. For the moment let it suffice to say only that active and passive rights are equally rights, and that neither as a class can be flatly said to be intrinsically more deserving of respect than the other.

Still another way of classifying rights is by the type of interest they protect. As we have seen, the price to be paid for protecting the interests of some persons is always the coercion of others, that is, violation of *their* interests. The state can only protect one man's interest by restricting the liberty of others by the imposition of duties. There is therefore a loss of liberty for every gain, an unhappy fact of life that requires legislators to rank interests in respect to worthiness or importance. Throughout its history the Anglo-American law has protected only those interests ranked near the top of such a scale; as our civilization becomes more crowded and

[8] The example is Salmond's. See Glanville Williams ed., *Salmond on Jurisprudence* (11th ed.), (London: Sweet & Maxwell, Ltd., 1957), p. 286.

complex, protection has been extended to a continually growing number of interests. The general tendency has been to create more passive rights at the expense of previously existing active rights. John Locke in the seventeenth century referred to three great classes of natural rights, the rights to "life, liberty, and property." The English law of his time protected the interests in bodily health and integrity, and physical survival ("life"), from physical force; the interest in free movement ("liberty") from actual restraint or imprisonment; and the interest in the exclusive use and enjoyment of one's money, land, and chattels ("property") from physical seizure, destruction, or fraud. Now, in the mid-twentieth century, the "right to life" means not only the right to health and survival, but also the right to enjoy life; this involves protection from certain forms of psychological as well as physical suffering, from the apprehension of injury as well as injury itself, from excessive noises, odors, and vibrations, and from invasions of personal privacy. The "right to property" now includes protection of "intangible" as well as tangible property: ideas, works of literature and art, good will, trade secrets, and reputation. The "right to liberty" now, as in the past, refers to the right to move about at will, but this active right has perforce retreated as the passive rights of life and property have advanced. Therefore, these other gains in rights have clearly been at the expense of Locke's "right to liberty."

3. RIGHTS AND DUTIES

It is often said that there can be no rights without duties, and that a prior condition for the acquisition or possession of rights is the ability and willingness to shoulder duties and responsibilities. The theory that acceptance of duties is the price any person must pay in order to have rights has been called[9] the doctrine of the *moral* correlation of rights and duties. This is in contradistinction to the doctrine of the *logical* correlation of rights and duties, to be considered below, which asserts that attribution of rights to one person logically entails the existence of at least one *other* person who has duties toward him. That a rightholder must himself have duties is by no means a logically necessary proposition. It is at least conceivable that a person should have a right to X but no correlative duty to provide or respect the X's of anyone else. Even though a rule conferring such an exceptional benefit might be morally repugnant, it would nevertheless be conceptually coherent. Indeed, if there is some reason for granting dutyless rights in certain cases so that the exemption is not arbitrary, then even the moral repugnance disappears. Some have claimed, for example, that since various animals can suffer pain, they have a right not to be mistreated,

9 S. I. Benn and R. S. Peters, *Social Principles and the Democratic State* (London: George Allen and Unwin Ltd., 1959), p. 89.

but since they are not rational beings, they lack the capacity to have duties. Animals would then constitute one kind of exception to the moral correlation doctrine, and perhaps human infants and idiots are other exceptions of the same kind.

What makes the moral correlation doctrine seem a plausible account of most legal rights is the fact that legal rights are conferred by general rules that apply to classes of persons rather than to individuals. Characteristically, the classes are so wide that many persons are members of both the class of rightholders and the class of those on whom are imposed the duties logically correlated with the conferred rights. Many rules of law, for example, apply to *all* citizens. Thus everyone has a right not to be physically beaten, which is correlated with the duties of everyone else not to beat him. Any arbitrarily selected John Doe will have the right in question, and also the correlated duty toward everyone else, both imposed by the same rule. That is only proper, but it is not logically necessary. A universal right not to be beaten that is correlated with duties imposed on everyone except John Doe would be a moral monstrosity but a logical possibility.

Even where rules are perfectly general and exceptionless, the rights and duties they give to any given person need not be related in such a way that the rights are conditional upon performance of the duties. Thus if Cain murders Abel, it does not necessarily follow that there is anybody whose duty not to kill Cain 's canceled. If Cain tortures Abel, to pick a more convincing example, it does not follow that Cain thereby forfeits his own right not to be tortured. That right should be unforfeitable under the governing rules.

That version of the moral correlativity doctrine that makes a man's rights conditional upon his exercise of corresponding duties to others is neither logically necessary nor morally desirable in every case. But there is no doubt that in a great many cases it is morally plausible. We send men to prison, and thereby deprive them of their rights of free movement, because they have not respected the rights of others; indeed, we tell them that their failure to discharge their duties has shown them unworthy of certain of their rights. Even in these cases, it is important to note that the criminal's invasion of his victim's rights did not absolve the *victim* of his corresponding duties to the criminal. The right of punishment is reserved to the state.

The doctrine of *logical* correlativity asserts not that a person's rights ought to be contingent upon performance of his own duties, but that his rights are necessarily linked with the duties of other people. This is not only a plausible doctrine, it is, for a certain class of rights and duties, logically unassailable, for as we have seen, legal claim-rights are *defined* in terms of other people's duties. A more general version of the logical correlativity thesis, however, encounters severe difficulties. I refer to the thesis that *all* duties entail other people's rights and *all* rights entail other people's duties.

Even if we confine our attention to legal contexts, there do seem prima facie to be some duties that are not correlated with the rights of others. Many duties of obedience imposed by legal rules are not "owed" to other persons, but rather to some wholly impersonal authority like "the law" or a painted stop sign. When a traffic signal directs me to stop, it is difficult to find an assignable person who can plausibly claim my stopping as his own due. The original legislators of the traffic ordinance may be long dead, and if vision is clear and no other motorists are in sight, there is no other person to whose right of way I owe respect. In short, I have a legal duty of obedience that is correlated with no other person's right against me.

When we leave legal contexts to consider moral obligations and other extralegal duties, a greater variety of duties without correlative rights present themselves. Duties of charity, for example, require us to contribute to one or another of a large number of eligible recipients, no one of whom can claim our contribution as his due. Charitable contributions are more like gratuitous services, favors, and gifts than repayments of debts or reparations, and yet we do have duties to be charitable. Many persons, moreover, believe they are required by their consciences to do more than the "duty" which *can* be demanded of them by their prospective beneficiaries.

That there now seem to be clear examples of duties without correlative rights is probably a consequence of the evolution of a new and generalized sense of the word "duty." Etymologically, the word is associated with actions that are *due* someone else, the payments of debts *to* creditors, the keeping of agreements with promisees, or the payment of club dues, legal fees, or tariff levies to appropriate authorities or their representatives. In this original sense, all duties are correlated with the rights of those *to* whom the duty is owed. On the other hand, there are numerous classes of duties, both legal and nonlegal, that are *not* logically correlated with the rights of other persons. This is probably a consequence of the fact that the word "duty" has come to be used for *any* action understood to be *required,* whether by the rights of others, or by law, or by higher authority, or by conscience. When the notion of requirement is in clear focus it is likely to seem the only essential element in the idea of duty, and the other component notion—that a duty is something *due* someone else—disappears. Thus, in this widespread but derivative usage, "duty" tends to be used for any action we feel we *must* (for whatever reason) do. It becomes, in short, a term of moral modality merely; and it is no wonder that the first thesis of the logical correlativity doctrine often fails.

What of the other side of the logical correlativity thesis that *all rights* entail other people's duties? Again, as long as we mean by "claim-right" a right which can be claimed *against* someone, it follows that all claim-rights are correlated with the duties of those against whom they may be claimed. There is another sense of "right," however, common in political manifestos if not in legal codes, and also closely linked to the notion of a claim, which provides us with some apparent exceptions to the logical correlativity thesis. In this "manifesto sense" of "right," to be discussed below, a right is a *claim to* something which need not also be a *claim against* anyone.

4. RIGHTS AND CLAIMS

Many philosophical writers have simply identified rights with claims. Dictionaries tend to define "claims," in turn, as "assertions of right," a dizzying piece of circularity that led one philosopher to complain, "We go in search of rights and are directed to claims, and then back again to rights in bureaucratic futility."[10] What then is the relation between a claim and a right?

As we shall see, a right is a kind of claim, and a claim is "an assertion of right," so a formal definition of either notion in terms of the other will not get us very far. Thus if we are after a "formal definition" of the usual philosophical sort, the game is over before it has begun, and we can say that the concept of a right is a "simple, undefinable, unanalyzable primitive." Here as elsewhere in philosophy this will have the effect of making the commonplace seem unnecessarily mysterious. We would be better advised not to attempt a formal definition of either "right" or "claim," but rather to use the idea of a claim in informal elucidation of the idea of a right. This is made possible by the fact that claiming is an elaborate sort of rule-governed activity. A claim is that which is claimed, the object of the act of claiming. If we concentrate on the whole activity of claiming, which is public, familiar, and open to our observation, rather than on its upshot alone, we may learn more about the generic nature of rights than we could ever hope to learn from a formal definition, even if one were possible.

Let us begin by distinguishing between: making claim to..., claiming that..., and having a claim. One sort of thing we may be doing when we claim is make claim to something, which means "to petition or seek by virtue of supposed right; to demand as due." Sometimes this is done by an acknowledged rightholder when he serves notice that he now wants turned over to him that which has already been acknowledged as his, such as something borrowed or improperly taken from him. The claim is often made by turning in a chit, a receipt, or a deed, that is, a title to something currently in the possession of someone else. On other occasions, making claim is making application for titles or rights themselves, as when a mining prospector stakes a claim to mineral rights, or a householder to a tract of land in the public domain, or an inventor to his patent rights. In the first kind of case, to make claim is to exercise rights one already has by present-

[10] H. B. Acton, "Symposium on 'Rights,'" *Proceedings of the Aristotelian Society* suppl. Vol. **XXIV** (1950), pp. 107–8.

ing title; in the other kind, it is to apply for the title itself by showing that one has satisfied conditions specified by a rule for the ownership of title and therefore can demand it as one's due.

Generally speaking, only the person who has a title or has qualified for it, or someone speaking in his name, can make claim to something as a matter of right. An important fact about rights (or claims) is that they can be claimed only by those who have them. Of course, anyone can claim *that* this umbrella is yours, but only you or your representative can actually claim the umbrella. If Smith owes Jones five dollars, only Jones can claim the five dollars as his own, although any bystander can *claim that* it belongs to Jones. One major difference between *making legal claim to* and *claiming that* is that the former is a legal performance with direct legal consequences, whereas the latter is often a mere piece of descriptive commentary with no legal force. Legally speaking, *making claim to* can itself make things happen. This sense of "claiming" might well be called the "performative sense," as opposed to "claiming that" (asserting in an especially insistent way), which can be called the "propositional sense." The legal power to claim (performatively) one's right or the things to which one has a right seems essential to the very notion of a legal right. A legal right to which one could not make claim (i.e., not even for official recognition) would be very "imperfect" indeed!

We come now to the third interesting employment of the claiming vocabulary, that involving not the verb "to claim" but the substantive "a claim." What is it to *have a claim* and how is this related to rights? I would like to suggest that *having a claim consists in being in a position to claim in the performative sense,* that is, *to make claim to.* If this suggestion is correct, it shows the primacy of the verbal over the nominative forms. It links claims to a kind of activity and obviates the temptation to think of claims as things, on the model of coins, pencils, and other material possessions which we can carry in our hip pockets. To be sure, we often make or establish our claims by presenting titles, which typically have the form of receipts, tickets, certificates, and other pieces of paper or parchment. The title, however, is not the same thing as the claim; rather it is the evidence that establishes the claim as valid. On this analysis, one might have a claim without ever claiming that to which one is entitled, or without even knowing that one has the claim. It is possible that one might simply be ignorant of the fact of being in a position to claim; or one might be unwilling to exploit that position for one reason or another, including fear that the legal machinery is broken down or corrupt and will not enforce one's claim despite its validity.

Nearly all writers maintain that there is some intimate connection between having a claim and having a right. Some identify right and claim without qualification; some define "right" as justified or justifiable claim, or recognized claim, or valid claim. My own preference is for the last definition. Some writers, however, reject the identification of rights with valid claims on the ground that all claims as such are valid, so that the expression "valid claim" is redundant. These writers would identify rights with claims *simpliciter*. But this is a very simple confusion. All claims are *put forward* as justified, whether they are justified in fact or not. A claim conceded even by its maker to have no validity is not a claim at all, but a mere demand. The highwayman, for example, demands his victim's money, but he hardly makes claim to it as rightfully his own. But it does not follow from this sound point that it is redundant to qualify claims as justified (or, as I prefer, valid) in the definition of a right, for not all claims put forward as valid really are valid; only the valid ones can be acknowledged as rights.

If having a valid claim is not redundant, i.e., if it is not redundant to pronounce *another's* claim valid, there must be such a thing as having a claim that is not valid. What would this be like? One might accumulate just enough evidence to argue with relevance and cogency that one has a right (or ought to be granted a right), although one's case might not be overwhelmingly conclusive. The argument might be strong enough to entitle one to a hearing and fair consideration. When one is in this position, it might be said that one "has a claim" that deserves to be weighed carefully. Nevertheless, the balance of reasons may turn out to militate against recognition of the claim, so that the claim is not a valid claim or right. Having a claim to X is not (yet) the same as having a right to X, but is rather *having a case,* consisting of relevant reasons of at least minimal plausibility, that one has a right to X. The case establishes a right, not to X, but to a fair hearing and consideration. Claims, so conceived, differ in degree: some are stronger than others. Rights, on the other hand, do not differ in degree; no one right is more of a right than another. That is the most important difference between rights and mere claims. It is analogous to the difference between *evidence* of guilt (subject to degrees of cogency) and *conviction* of guilt (which is all or nothing). One can "have evidence" that is not conclusive just as one can "have a claim" that is not valid.

Another reason for not identifying rights with claims *simply* is that there is a well-established usage in international law and politics that makes a theoretically interesting distinction between claims and rights. Statesmen are sometimes led to speak of "claims" when they are concerned with the natural needs of deprived human beings in conditions of scarcity. Young orphans everywhere in the world *need* good upbringings, balanced diets, education, and technical training, but unfortunately there are many places where those goods are in such short supply that it is impossible to provide them for all who need them. If we persist in speaking of those needs as constituting rights and not merely claims, we are committed to the conception of a right which is an entitlement *to* some good, but not a valid claim *against* any particular individual, for in conditions of scarcity there may be no determinate individuals who can plausibly be said to have a duty to provide the missing goods to those in need. J.E.S. Fawcett prefers to keep the distinction between claims and rights firmly in mind. "Claims," he writes, "are needs and demands in movement, and there is a continuous transformation as a society advances [toward greater abundance] of economic and social claims into civil and political rights...and not all countries or all claims are by any means at the same stage in the process."[11] Manifesto writers on the other side who seem to identify needs, or at least basic needs, with what they call "human rights," are more properly described, I think, as urging upon the world community the moral principle that *all* basic human needs ought to be recognized as *claims* (in the customary prima facie sense) worthy of sympathy and serious consideration right now, even though, in many cases, they cannot yet plausibly be treated as valid claims, that is, as grounds of any other people's duties.

For all of that, I still have a certain sympathy with the manifesto writers, and am even willing to speak of a special "manifesto sense" of "right," in which a right need not be correlated with another's duty. Natural needs are real claims, if only upon hypothetical future beings not yet in existence. I accept the moral principle that to have an unfulfilled need is to have a kind of claim against the world, even if against no one in particular. A natural need for some good as such, like a natural desert, is always a reason in support of a claim to that good. A person in need, then, is always "in a position" to make a claim, even when there is no one in the corresponding position to do anything about it. Such claims, based on need alone, are "permanent possibilities of rights," the natural seed from which rights grow. Manifesto writers are easily forgiven for speaking of them as if they are already actual rights, for this is but a powerful way of expressing the conviction that they ought to be recognized by states as potential rights and consequently as determinants of present aspirations and guides to present policies. That usage, I think, is a valid exercise of rhetorical license.

I prefer to define rights as valid claims rather than justified ones, because I suspect that justification is too broad a qualification. "Validity," as I understand it, is justification of a peculiar and narrow kind, namely justification within a system of rules. A man has a legal right when the official recognition of his claim (as valid) is called for by the governing rules. This definition, of course, hardly applies to moral rights, but that is not because the genus of which moral rights are a species is something other than claims. A man has a moral right when he has a claim, the recognition of which is called for—not (necessarily) by legal rules—but by moral principles, or the principles of an enlightened conscience.

11 J. E. S. Fawcett, "The International Protection of Human Rights," in *Political Theory and the Rights of Man,* ed. D. D. Raphael (Bloomington: Indiana University Press, 1967), pp. 125, 128.

CHAPTER FIVE

Conflicts
of Legal Rights

1. CONFLICTS OF CLAIMS
There is no reason why a legal claim possessed by one citizen cannot conflict with a legal claim possessed by another. Having a claim, as we have seen, is something like "having a point," or "having a case," or even "having a complaint." It consists in having relevant reasons of some weight that put one in a position to *make* claim to something. These reasons, were they to be put forward, would tend to support a claim and lend it credence and cogency, even if, in the end, they should fail to *establish* the claim and compel its recognition. Having a case is better than having no case at all, but it can be somewhat less than having a decisive or conclusive case. Claims, then, can differ in degree; some are stronger than others. When Doe and Roe both have claims to X which are such that not both can be granted or recognized, then their claims can be said to be in conflict. A judge may decide that while both competing claims are plausible enough to deserve a hearing, neither is strong enough to be recognized cr declared valid, or he may decide that only one is valid. In either event, the conflict of claims remains but does not grow into anything stronger. The law remains consistent and gives no sanction to socially disruptive combat. It would be otherwise, however, if the court were to declare that *both* conflicting claims were *valid*.

2. LEVELS OF GENERALITY IN STATEMENTS OF RIGHTS

When two specific claims of precise particularity are both declared valid, conflict between them seems quite intolerable. Thus, Grunt's right to the exclusive possession and control of ten acres at Blackacre is logically inconsistent with Groan's right to the exclusive possession and control of precisely the same ten acres. Before considering whether such conflicting rights can be allowed to coexist in the same legal system, it would be wise to distinguish levels of generality in the statement of rights, for what applies to singular statements ascribing or conferring particular rights to particular persons may not apply without qualification to statements ascribing or conferring more general rights.

(i) SPECIFIC RIGHTS

On the lowest level of generality are statements ascribing to specific persons the right either to *do* specific actions at a specified time and place, or to *have* specific objects in their possession or control for a specified time, or to *be* in a certain precisely described condition for a specified time. Thus, John Doe has a right to cast his vote in secret for Richard Roe when his turn arrives at the polls in the first precinct, second ward, any time between 8:00 A.M. and 8:00 P.M. on November 5; Arnold Abel has a right to possess the wallet that is now in his pocket; Henry Hooch has the right to be quietly drunk tomorrow night at midnight within the confines of his own home.

(ii) DISCRETIONARY RIGHTS

When a person has a legal duty to do that which he also has a specific right to do, then of course the law gives him no discretion to decide whether he shall do it. He is legally compelled to do that which he has a specific right to do, and indeed he has a right only in the minimal sense of a valid claim against others not to prevent him from performing his duty. Many writers reserve the term "right" for the more interesting cases in which entitlement is more than the permission trivially entailed by duty. In those cases, specific rights are themselves instances of more general rights possessed by the rightholders. Doe has the right to vote not only for Roe (his favorite) but for any candidate he wishes; Abel has the right to dispose of his cash as he pleases; Hooch is king in his own home, which is legally his "castle." Any American citizen in New York has the (specific) right to travel to Chicago on the next plane in virtue of his (discretionary) right to go wherever he pleases; a man's right to worship at a Roman Catholic church follows from his more general right to worship at a "church of his choice." Within a certain area of autonomy, the rightholder may do anything he wishes. Such rights are, in effect, legal competencies; they certify that within a given area, subject to certain limits, it is John Doe and no one else who decides what is to be done.

Discretionary rights may vary in degree of generality, for at least two reasons. First, Doe's discretionary right may be a right to do whatever he pleases in *area X,* in which case the generality of the right will be a function of the size of *area X.* Thus, Doe's right to *do* whatever he wishes is more general than Roe's right to *say* whatever he wishes. Since saying is but one kind of doing, one right is contained in the other. Second, Doe's discretionary right may be disjunctive in form, conferring upon him the discretion to do either *X, Y,* or *Z* as he chooses, that is, to choose among some limited set of alternatives of a number greater than one. In this case, the generality of the right will depend upon the number of alternatives permitted. If Doe may buy any kind of automobile he wishes, his right is more general (i.e., his discretion more broad) than Roe's if Roe may buy only an American made car. Another thing to note about discretionary rights is that among the alternatives they often permit is the right to perform *no action at all.* The rights to worship at a church of one's choice and to vote for a candidate of one's choice include the specific rights not to worship and not to vote.

(iii) RIGHT-PACKAGES

Various discretionary rights are often grouped together and given a common name. We can refer to sets of discretionary rights all relating to some particular activity or subject matter as "right-packages." Thus, Abel's "right to a fair trial" consists of the discretionary right to call witnesses in his own defense, the discretionary right of nonself-incrimination, the discretionary right of cross-examination, and many other rights related to the conduct of a trial and considered together. Similarly, Baker's "civil rights" consist of a right to vote, to use public facilities, and so on.

(iv) RIGHT-CATEGORIES

These are classification labels for rights of any of the first three types, classified (usually) according to the general kind of interest protected. "Personal rights," for example, are sometimes distinguished from "proprietary rights," and "civic rights" from "economic rights." These are categories in which right-packages can be placed, as well as the discretionary rights that make up right-packages and the specific rights entailed by discretionary rights.

(v) RIGHT-NAMES

These are all expressions of the form "The right to. . . ." Right-names can apply to *kinds of discretionary rights* ("The right to call witnesses," "The right to worship at a church of one's choice"), *kinds of right-packages* ("The right to a fair trial," "The right to the free exercise of one's religion"), *right-categories* ("The right to life," "The right to property"), or *ideal directives* addressed to those in appropriate positions to do their best for a particular kind of human value, such as life, liberty, or property ownership. Many references to the grand old rights to life, liberty, property, the pursuit of happiness, and so on, in manifestos, constitutions, and philosophical discussions are best understood as allusions to ideal directives, even though masquerading as right-names of some other kind. "The right to life" may appear, at first sight, to be another relatively specific right like the right to vote. Despite its singular title, however, it is rarely taken to be one specific right or even one narrow class of rights among others. Often the right to life is plausibly construed as a broad right-category in which a large miscellany of rights can be placed, some of them negative (for example, the right not to be killed by others without due process or just cause) and some of them positive (for example the rights to those goods indispensable to a life "worth living," that is, to a form of vital existence a good deal higher than the merely vegetative). But to acknowledge that all persons have rights in this category is not yet saying much about what these rights are, or about what rights are entailed by universal possession of something called "the right to life." For this reason, commitment to this universal right is often best understood as an endorsement of a more or less vague ideal.

Whether or not "the right to life" rules out capital punishment, mercy killing, abortion, or wartime conscription; which of the admitted goods of life are to count as necessary to a life worth living; which impositions of risk to life are to be graded severe enough to count as takings of life; which causes for taking life are just: these are questions whose rival answers are all compatible with the universal right to life. Acknowledgment of this universal right commits us to the view that human life is a precious thing to be protected by law whenever possible and by whatever means are reasonable, but it does not, by itself, entail the existence of any specific rights of specific persons, nor does it, by itself, commit judges and legislators to any particular resolution of its marginal perplexities. It is not the name of a particular package of valid claims; rather it is an ideal directive to legislative aspiration, commanding us to do our best for the cause of human life as we judge the various claims that may be before us in our roles as legislators, judges, and moral agents. Similar analyses can be given of "the right to liberty" and "the right to property."

3. CONFLICTS BETWEEN RIGHTS (VALID CLAIMS)   It should be no surprise that general rights in the sense of "ideal directives" are in chronic conflict both internally and with each other. "The right to life" is in internal conflict when soldiers must die so that their buddies may live, or when a famine overwhelms food supplies. "The right to liberty" conflicts with itself when demand for passage exceeds transportation facilities and some must wait in order that others may go, as when the moving of a house obstructs a highway. Recognition of "the right to property" does not help resolve the conflict between a factory owner's right to use his property for his own benefit and a neighbor's right to the peaceful and quiet enjoyment of his land. Similarly, the right to life conflicts with the right to liberty when authorities must decide whether to quarantine whole neighborhoods to prevent the spread of a plague. "In a famine one man's right to life may well involve infringement, by the commandeering of food hoards, of another's right to property."[1] The right to liberty may conflict with the right to property when public movement through an area is made unreasonably slow and difficult by a combination of natural obstacles, congested conditions, and "inviolable" private land. In all these cases, the conflicting principles referred to by the right-names are so usefully vague and flexible that conflict is easily tolerated. If the "rights" in question are merely directives to adjudicators to do their best for certain kinds of human interests, they may be satisfied by a give and take of intelligent adjustments and mutual accommodations. This can be done without sacrifice or compromise of the commitment to do our best by all of the important values involved. Our "best," in some cases, will unhappily not be very much.

Apparent conflicts between specific valid claims are more serious matters. When both Abel and Baker have a valid claim to exclusive possession of the same object at the same time, their claims cannot be *rights,* for they entail no correlative duties in the other to forbear. Conflict automatically reduces the claims to *liberties.* Each may do his best to exclude the other, and the state will not intervene. When both are prepared to fight, however, the result will be that kind of violent struggle between equally right and equally self-righteous gladiators that no civil society can long tolerate. Conflict between equally valid competencies will have the same unhappy result whenever the rightholders choose to exercise their discretion in the same way.

A legal system cannot very well countenance conflicting specific rights. Normally courts avoid such conflict by redefining the boundaries of the conflicting claims, either by writing express exceptive clauses into the claims to make them mutually consistent, or (more commonly) by "finding" such clauses implicit in the rules that conferred the rights on the contending parties. By virtue of such processes, rights become more complex. The full statement of any legal right, no matter how simple its name or brief its description, will often include numerous exceptive clauses, many of which are themselves qualified by further exceptive clauses, and so on. It may even be that no legal right has its boundaries fixed and stable for all time, that new and unanticipated conflicts with other rights may at any time require sharper specification of boundary lines via the method of appended exceptive clauses.

Imagine a simple legal system at an early and immature stage that con-

---

1 S. I. Benn and R. S. Peters, *Social Principles and the Democratic State* (London: George Allen and Unwin Ltd., 1959), p. 96.

tains a rule granting everybody the right to move his arms through space in whatever direction and velocity he pleases, and also a rule granting everyone the right not to be punched in the nose. Nip then punches Tuck in the nose and claims in court that he was well within his rights, while Tuck claims with equally righteous conviction that his right was violated. If the relevant statutes contain no exceptive clauses and there are no relevant precedents, the court will have to make a decision about how these inconsistent statutes are to be interpreted. The court may turn to records of the deliberations of the legislature that passed the statutes in an effort to divine the original intentions of the lawmakers, or it may unabashedly "make law," that is, further refine and specify existing law on its own. In either case, it is likely to have recourse to the same sort of interest-balancing procedures that often guide the deliberations of legislators. It will find that the defendant was promoting a private interest in the free and vigorous motion of his limbs, but that his victim's private interest in freedom from facial pain and injury was more important to him than the competing interest was to the defendant. Evidence may be adduced to show that most or even all people who have both interests weigh the facial interest more heavily than the limb interest. Moreover, the court may discover a public interest in protecting faces (preventing medical expenses, vendettas, lost man hours) that is heavier than a public interest in promoting vigorous arm motion. Consequently, it may restrict the free motion right by an appropriate exceptive clause protecting faces, and its new rule will be binding on subsequent courts. In such a way, the boundaries between rights, while always in some degree of flux, become relatively fixed and stable; away from the boundaries, within each right's "central core," there will be more and more security.

4. PRIMA-FACIE RIGHTS

There is no way of drawing the boundaries of all individual legal rights so tightly that we can dispense with the need for judgment when conflicts threaten. Accommodation must often be worked out after the fact of conflict rather than prevented in advance by rules and decrees. This has led some theorists to proclaim that all legal discretionary rights are, in the very nature of the case, *provisional*. On this view, it is tacitly understood that recognition of a right can always be withdrawn or qualified when necessary to permit satisfaction of a conflicting claim. There are no "absolute" rights which always have the right of way when collisions threaten. Put another way, "the right to X" is always to be understood as "the right to X *unless* some stronger claim shows up," the "unless clause" being tacitly understood. According to this theory, since there is no foolproof way of knowing when a stronger claim will turn up, reliance upon our rights should always be tempered with skepticism; a right is no ironclad guarantee. Possession of a discretionary right creates only a *presumption* in a given case at a given time that one also has a specific right normally derivable from it.

Many writers call a merely presumptive right a "prima-facie right," and oppose it, in meaning, to the "absolute" right that a person can possess unconditionally. The right that people have to exchange ideas freely, according to Richard Brandt, is a prima-facie right. The ascription of that right is properly translated thus: "People have a right (in the strong [absolute] sense) to exchange ideas freely if and whenever no conflicting more urgent moral considerations stand in the way."[2] When more urgent conflicting considerations are not present, the prima-facie right becomes an absolute right, that is, the presumption of an absolute right becomes conclusive. However, the presumption is subject to immediate weakening the moment circumstances change, so that absolute rights lapse back into prima-facie ones, and formerly conclusive presumptions are overturned. What cannot be overturned, on this view, is possession of the prima-facie right as such. One continues to have *a* claim, no matter what happens; no one can take *that* away. The validity of the claim, however, comes and goes with the changing circumstances.

Upon consideration, the theory that all legal rights are prima facie in the sense explained seems highly paradoxical. The basis of the distinction between "having a claim" and "having a valid claim" is that mere claims differ in strength and hence are subject to defeat by rival claims, whereas validity is not a property that can vary in degree. In respect to their validity, all genuine rights are equal. But if *all* valid claims are merely presumptive, their validity does not distinguish them in kind from those "mere claims" that are understood to have a merely presumptive character, and a useful distinction is undermined. Similarly, the basis of the distinction between rights and "mere privileges" is thrown in doubt if all rights are, like revocable privileges, subject to the withdrawal at any time of legal recognition. Yet, for all these misgivings based on the utility of ordinary distinctions, there remains the fact upon which the theory of prima-facie rights is based, namely, the apparent impossibility in a world full of conflict of treating any right as an unconditional guarantee.

Perhaps the way out of this dilemma, at least in respect to legal rights, is to take seriously the distinction between recognition and enforcement. The state's promise of enforcement to any given rightholder cannot be totally unconditional, but perhaps its recognition of the validity of rightholders' claims *can* be totally unconditional (or at least much closer to being so than the promise of enforcement). Unconditional recognition does have some value, after all, even if it does not prevent infringement in every conceivable circumstance, for it certifies a feature that we all take to be essential

---

[2] Richard B. Brandt, *Ethical Theory* (Englewood Cliffs, N.J.: Prentice-Hall, Inc., 1959), p. 437.

to rights, whether in conflict or not—that they are not something that one has only at specific moments, only to lose, regain, and lose again as circumstances shift. Rights are themselves *property,* things we own, and from which we may not even temporarily be dispossessed. Perhaps in some circumstances rights may be rightfully infringed, but that is quite different from their being taken away and then returned.

A less paradoxical alternative to the theory of prima-facie rights is the view that a person can maintain a right to X even when he is not morally justified in its exercise, or others are justified in not according it to him. Lack of moral justification for exercising a right does not entail (even temporary) nonpossession. Moreover, it is possible to have a duty but, because of conflicting duties and other moral considerations, also to have a moral justification for not acting in accordance with it. There is no contradiction in saying of a person that he *ought* not to perform one of his duties. The right correlated with that duty remains a right, even when honored in the breech.

It may seem paradoxical to say that it can sometimes be right not to give a man his due (what he deserves or has a right to), for that is to say that it can be right to treat a man unjustly. But that, in fact, is precisely the final moral of the rejection of the theory of prima-facie rights. The realm of justice is not the whole of morality, and even within its spacious domain, certified injustice is unavoidable. This is an unpleasant fact of life that every moralist must accommodate. To deny that a rightly violated right could have been a real right at all is to deny this fact of life, and to do so in a way that can only encourage injustice, whether necessary or not, and discourage the spirit of reluctance, apology, and respect that should attend even justified or necessary injustice. I cannot forbear, in conclusion, quoting at length from Herbert Morris, who puts this point eloquently:

It may be justifiable not to accord a man his rights; it may be right not to; it may be justifiable infringing his rights. But it is no less a wrong to *him,* no less an infringement. It is seriously misleading to turn all justifiable infringements into non-infringements by saying that the right is only *prima-facie,* as if we have in concluding that we should not accord a man his rights, made out a case that he had none. To use the language of *prima-facie* rights misleads, for it suggests that a presumption of the existence of a right has been overcome in these cases where all that can be said is that the presumption in favor of according a man his rights has been overcome.[3]

Still, the point of the prima-facie right theorists may tell when put in another way. When they speak about prima-facie rights they talk in a manner appropriate to *ideal directives,* not to specific and discretionary rights; mere presumptiveness is not unbecoming in a guiding ideal, though it be fatal to the very existence of an established right.

3 Herbert Morris, "Persons and Punishment," *The Monist* (October 1968), p. 499.

5. TRANSCATEGORIAL CONFLICTS How can conflicts between legal rights, which are intolerable in any legal system aspiring to consistency, be obviated, or, failing that, be resolved? In some cases, relatively clear rules can be formulated for determining the right of way in anticipation of right-collisions. More typically, however, our question calls for the formulation of *policy* for dealing with conflicts in the absence of precise rules. When there are applicable rules for determining the right of way in a given case, the colliding interests cannot both be treated as rights. If the rule states that all cars may proceed carefully through inter-sections but that red cars always have precedence over blue ones, then the driver of a blue car has a general right to proceed through intersections *unless* a red car is doing the same, and *that* right (so qualified) is not in conflict with the right of the red car driver. (Subordination is not a form of conflict!) The blue car driver simply has no right against the red car driver in the first place. Many conflict situations, however, are much more complicated than this, and therefore not subject to a priori resolutions via the application of simple right of way rules.

Formulation of policies for dealing with the more complex conflicts necessarily requires assessment of the protected interests involved. The diffi-culty is that we often cannot say in a general way which interests are the weightiest. It is hard enough balancing types of interests in the abstract, when we speak of "the Interest (with a capital I) in something" as if it were an impersonal entity belonging to no one in particular, but it becomes more difficult still when we must weigh the conflicting interests of particular persons in particular cases without knowing how heavily they sit on the scale. In these cases, we are not out to determine how heavy a given Interest is generally, but how heavy an interest of a given general kind is when it belongs to a particular litigant in a particular case. Insofar as we think that certain kinds of conflict can be obviated by simple "right of way" rules, the formulation of such rules might best be understood as a task for an ideal legislature. When the type of conflict seems to require instead policies for the guidance of interest balancing in particular cases, perhaps the cautious philosopher should think of it as a question for some "ideal court."

Conflicts between personal and property rights are especially controversial examples of transcategorial conflict. It is sometimes said that in a conflict between a property right and a personal (i.e., nonproperty) right, the personal right always has precedence. This generalization, which makes about as much sense as the assertion that red things are always heavier than green things, is usually made by people who have taken category labels far too seriously. It is not difficult to think of circumstances in which a specific personal right belonging to John Doe should be given priority over a specific property right belonging to Richard Roe, but it is equally easy to think of examples where the priority relation is reversed. Doe's ownership

of a lot and house confers on him the right to possess, enjoy, use, or dispose of it as he sees fit; but if he sees fit to use it in such a way as to cause a widespread and nauseating stench, nerve-shattering noise, or dangerous pitfalls on the adjacent public streets, his property rights are subject to justifiable delimitation in order to protect what may be more important personal (and property) rights of neighbors and passersby. On the other hand, it is perfectly clear that Mr. and Mrs. Doe have the right to make love to one another. Yet, if they choose to exercise this right in Mr. Roe's flower beds, their neighbor's property rights take precedence.

Can it not be said that rights of the one category are "on the whole" more important than rights of the other? Even this is probably too broad a generalization to sustain, and in any case it is insufficiently precise to have any utility. Suppose we could give every specific property right and every specific personal right a "score" and place it in a ranking order on some common scale of "importance." What could we expect to find? Our examples suggest that specific instances of each type of right would be interspersed throughout with instances of the other kind. It would be very much like ranking human beings of different races, sexes, or classes in respect to scores on an objective test of intelligence, strength, or resistance to disease. Even if one group should have a heavier concentration of scores at the top end of the scale and a sparser concentration at the lower end, making its average score or position higher, we could still expect a large degree of overlap in the distribution. For example, it might even be possible that the poorer group "on the whole" contributed the individual with the single highest score, and the better group "on the whole" contributed the individual with the single lowest score. It would be otherwise if we were comparing all human beings with (say) all chimpanzees. In that case we could expect to find that the poorest human score would still be above the highest chimp score, and that a substantial gap would separate the two. If the grading of rights came out that way, so that the most trivial personal right was still more important than the most serious property right, or if there were only a tiny amount of overlap rather than general interdispersion, then the results would be of considerable utility, and transcategorial conflicts, with only a few well-known exceptions, could all be resolved in the same way. But nobody's ranking of rights, either his own or others', comes out that simply.

Still, it is possible for like-minded persons to agree that particular narrowly described subclasses of rights in one category are *always* to be treated as more important than certain precisely described subclasses of rights in another category. Legislators, for example, may agree that everyone has a right to do X except when doing X would infringe someone else's right to do Y. This is, in effect, to direct that all conflicts in the future between rights to X and rights to Y are to be resolved uniformly in favor of Y. More precisely, since this is achieved by a new *law,* the rights themselves have been redefined so that they no longer *can* conflict. There no longer is such a thing as a right to do X simply, for it has been replaced by a "right to do X except when it would prevent others from doing Y," and that new right obviously cannot be in conflict with anyone's right to do Y.

Before the passage of the Civil Rights Act of 1964, any American Negro who wished to drive his family from (say) Washington, D.C., to Jackson, Mississippi, ran the risk of severe inconvenience and even danger. Because highway facilities were by local custom segregated, he could not anticipate when it would be necessary to drive miles out of his way to find a "public" rest room, a place to eat, or, more importantly, lodgings for the night. Owners of gas stations, restaurants, and motels had the legal right to solicit, accept, or exclude customers as they saw fit, and most of them saw fit to exercise their property rights by excluding all Negroes. Since passage of the Civil Rights Law, things must be described differently. Southern homeowners still have the right (derived from their ownership) to exclude anyone from their property, but those who are permitted to serve the public by providing food and lodgings in exchange for money must serve *all* the public or none at all. (More exactly, their exclusions cannot be merely arbitrary.) Their former right to exclude anyone at all from their property has now been replaced by the right to exclude anyone *except* those applying for licensed and advertised services (and who are not drunk, disorderly, and so on). Congress decided that a motorist's right not to be excluded on arbitrary grounds from hotels and restaurants along public highways is *always* more important than the innkeeper's right to serve whomever he pleases. Hence the latter right was changed in such a way that it can never conflict with the former.

This sort of legislative carving of an exception out of a previously existing right bears some resemblance to what is often done by private rightholders themselves through contracts and other special legal devices. "Thus the right of a landowner may be subject to, and limited by, that of a tenant to the temporary use of the property; or to the right of a mortgagee to sell or take possession; or to the right of a neighboring landowner to the use of a way or other easement; or to the right of the vendor of land in respect of restrictive covenants entered into by the purchaser as to the use of it; for example, a covenant not to build upon it."[4] The right in these examples that "limits or derogates from some more general right belonging to some other person"[5] is called by lawyers an *encumbrance,* or "right over the property of someone else." An encumbrance upon another person's right may be itself subject to another encumbrance, as when a tenant sublets; in principle there is no reason why the process cannot go on indefinitely. What

4 John Salmond, *Jurisprudence,* 11th ed., ed. Glanville Williams (London: Sweet & Maxwell Ltd., 1957), p. 294.
5 Salmond, *Jurisprudence,* p. 294.

is important for present purposes is that an encumbrance on a right is not a conflict between the rights of different parties, but an agreed method for redrawing right-boundaries, at least temporarily, so as to prevent conflict.

Legislatively restricted rights and encumbranced rights, even though they can be described as rights with exceptive clauses, are not the same as so-called "prima-facie" rights, and are not vulnerable to the same objections. A restricted or encumbranced right is a right to do X except in certain definitely and exhaustively described circumstances, whereas a prima-facie right is a right to do X except when there is "some more urgent moral consideration," its nature unspecified and open-ended, that stands in the way.

6. THE CONCEPT OF AN ABSOLUTE CONSTITUTIONAL RIGHT

A controversy has raged in recent years over whether constitutional rights, especially those guaranteed by the First Amendment, should be interpreted by the courts as "absolute." Many First Amendment cases were decided by the U.S. Supreme Court in the period from 1959–1962 over the eloquent dissents of Justice Hugo Black, the leading spokesman for the "absolutist" position. Justice Black in one case insisted that "the First Amendment means what it says."[6] What the First Amendment *says* is:

Congress shall make no law respecting an establishment of religion, or prohibiting the free exercise thereof; or abridging the freedom of speech, or of the press; or the right of the people peaceably to assemble, and to petition the Government for a redress of grievances.

"I read 'no law...abridging,' " said Justice Black, "to mean *no law abridging*,"[7] which is to say (he makes clear) that the First Amendment prohibition is complete, exceptionless, and unconditional: "...the principles of the First Amendment are stated in precise and mandatory terms and unless they are applied in those terms, the freedoms of religion, speech, press, assembly, and petition will have no effective protection."[8]

The opposing position, and the one that actually prevailed in the early 1960's, is most frequently associated with the late Justice Felix Frankfurter. In this view, there are no absolute rights, even in the First Amendment, and when the interest protected by a constitutional right conflicts with a weightier interest in public safety or public order, the courts must permit infringement of the right. In one free speech case, Frankfurter declared that "The demands of free speech in a democratic society as well as the interest in national security are better served by candid and informed weighing of the

---

6 Barenblatt v. United States, 360 U.S. 109, 143–44 (1959). Dissenting opinion.

7 Smith v. California, 361 U.S. 147, 157 (1959). Concurring opinion.

8 Wilkinson v. United States, 365 U.S. 399, 422–23 (1961). Dissenting opinion.

competing interests, within the confines of the judicial process, than by announcing dogmas too inflexible for the...problems to be solved."[9] The alternative to inflexible dogmas is the method of ad hoc "interest-balancing." Even when a judicially recognized constitutional right is on one side of the balance, it might be invaded or even "infringed" when the interest on the other side more than balances it:

We agree that compulsory disclosure of the names of an organization's members may in certain instances infringe constitutionally protected rights of association.... But to say this much is only to recognize one of the points of reference from which analysis must begin....Against the impediments which particular governmental regulation causes to entire freedom of individual action, there must be weighed the value to the public of the end which the regulation may achieve.[10]

It is of course beyond the scope of this work to decide whether any American constitutional rights *are* absolute. The philosophically prior question is: How *could* a right be "absolute?" What can it *mean* to say of a right that it is absolute? One source of confusion can be eliminated by a distinction between a right's *scope* and its degree of *incumbency* within that scope. It is plain that such First Amendment rights as free speech cannot be unlimited in scope; no one can expect the courts to guarantee his "right" to say anything, any time, any place. If there were such a right there could be no law of defamation, no protection against fraud, no penalty for solicitation to crime, and, in short, no protection of other rights as vital to private and public interests as free speech itself. Consequently, various implicit exceptive clauses must be understood as part of the rule that spells out the right to free speech. Some of these clauses presumably were understood at the time the First Amendment was adopted, for there was even then a well-developed body of law on defamation, fraud, incitement, and solicitation. Other exceptions have no doubt developed slowly through the piecemeal evolution of the common law and forced judicial clarifications of borderline cases. As a result, the boundaries of the right's domain have become reasonably clear and stable, though there may still be occasional waverings, and controversial marginal cases on both sides of the boundaries may always exist.

First Amendment rights, then, are not "absolute" in the sense of "unlimited in scope": the scope of free speech must necessarily be narrower than the range of all possible speech. But that is no reason why these rights, as qualified by exceptive clauses, cannot be absolute in the sense of laying *unconditionally incumbent* duties of respect and enforcement upon the courts. A rule with exceptive clauses may itself have no exceptions. A First Amendment right, in short, may be limited in extent by the definitions of established judicial rules, yet be unconditionally obligatory within its proper

[9] Dennis v. United States, 341 U.S. 524–25 (1951).
[10] Communist Party v. Subversive Activities Control Board, 367 U.S. 190–91 (1961).

domain. The courts would decide whether a given exercise of free speech, for example, falls *clearly* within the boundaries of First Amendment protection; if it does, then any statute that prohibits it, or any governmental action that restricts it, must be declared unconstitutional. If the speech in question falls in the vague no man's land near the right's wavering boundaries, the court must further clarify the law and fix its boundaries by whatever procedures of constitutional interpretation (perhaps including "interest-balancing") are open to it. But once having pronounced the act in question to be within the area of constitutional protection, on the intelligible "absolutistic" view we are considering, it is no longer open to the court to "weigh" that protection against other considerations, for the constitution says that its guaranteed rights, once correctly determined, always have more weight than any possible combination of opposing interests, private or public.

The "defining of absolutes" method is possible only in a legal system of sufficient maturity to have reasonably settled boundary lines, established after much conflict and redefinition through explicit and implicitly understood exceptive clauses, between the various rights it confers. The method presupposes that each right, no matter how vague its boundaries at the periphery, has a central core of clear and certain cases that are (unless resort is made to constitutional amendment) permanently and unconditionally established. Thus, it is always open to an American citizen, without any question, to express in speech or writing his opinion that a policy of his government is unwise, unjust, or otherwise mistaken, or his opinion as to "what the public welfare requires."[11] It is unconditionally open to an American to receive without interference the sacraments of his church, or to have some time and place to engage in prayer or worship, or simply to be a member of a church. These activities are at the "hard core" of the free exercise of religion right, well away from the boundaries with other rights, unrestricted by legislated exceptive clauses, and unencumbranced.

Laurent Frantz has pointed out that some constitutional rights other than those in the First Amendment are universally accepted as absolutely unconditional in their central core cases. If an accused person is to be denied the right to counsel, the Constitution will have to be amended first, for its guarantee is not subject to judicial overruling as a result of "interest-balancing" in a given case. It is simply not open to courts to balance a clearly defined and acknowledged right against *any* interests, even those in public safety and public welfare. If, on the other hand, a court could weigh interests against acknowledged core cases of constitutional rights, case by case, then the results might be contrary to everyone's present understanding:

Defendants in criminal cases can be tried in secret, or held incommunicado without trial, can be denied knowledge of the accusation against them, and the right to

11 Laurent B. Frantz, "The First Amendment in the Balance," *Yale Law Journal*, LXXI (1962), 1438.

counsel, and the right to call witnesses in their own defense, and the right to trial by jury. Ex post facto laws and bills of attainder can be passed. Habeas corpus can be suspended, though there is neither rebellion nor invasion. Private property can be taken for public use without just, or any, compensation. Suffrage qualifications based on sex or race can be reinstituted. Anything which the Constitution says *cannot* be done *can* be done, if Congress thinks and the Court agrees (or is unwilling to set aside the congressional judgment) that the interests thereby served outweighed those which were sacrificed. Thus the whole idea of a government of limited powers, and of a written constitution as a device for attaining that end, is at least potentially at stake.[12]

Are these hard core rights *never,* under any conceivable circumstances, abridgeable? (They are of course subject to change by constitutional amendment, but that is another matter.) Is an individual to be given his rights even if the whole public safety or welfare must be sacrificed in the process, or national independence lost as a consequence? Would it not be better in extreme emergencies, where all that is precious rides on what we do, to deny a given individual his opinion, his sacrament, his trial by jury? *Better,* perhaps, or wiser, or more prudent, or even more justifiable on the whole, but still a desperate emergency measure, like the amputation of a limb. It would be the sacrifice of legality itself, of justice, of an undenied right, for the sake of something held even more important. Perhaps courts *ought* to infringe rights in desperate circumstances, but that can never be their understood legal function. If or when judges take such desperate extralegal steps, their actions are special, ad hoc, and presumably sorrowful infringements or suspensions of rights, not the authoritative redefining of right-boundaries, or the official denial that a right existed in the first place. "One's need for a new car," wrote Frantz, "may be balanced against the other uses to which the same money might be put but not against 'Thou shalt not steal.' "[13] In truly extraordinary circumstances, one might conceivably be justified, in one's own conscience, in stealing another's car, but that justification doesn't affect the shape of the other's property rights. A justified violation of another's legal rights is still a violation of his rights, which one can never have a legal right to do. The point applies even to violations by courts of law.

A guaranteed *right,* "absolute" within its established sphere, adds something of great importance to a liberty, or a "mere privilege," or a "right" that is vulnerable to overturning by interest-balancing procedures. When the government leaves me at liberty (merely) to do X, it tells me in effect that I may do X if I can, but it will not protect me by imposing a duty of noninterference upon others. A liberty is a permission without a protection. A "mere privilege" may or may not add protection to the permission. When it does, the privilege looks more like a right than like a mere liberty. Unlike

[12] Frantz, "The First Amendment in the Balance," 1445.
[13] Frantz, "The First Amendment in the Balance," 1440.

rights, however, neither the permission nor the continued protection are assured; either can be withdrawn at any time at the state's pleasure, although the holder of a privilege will be warned in advance that withdrawal is coming. It would be otherwise with a so-called "nonabsolute right." When the government grants me a "right" that is vulnerable to interest-balancing tests even at its core, it tells me, in effect, that I may do X and others may not interfere, *but* that this permission cum protection does not apply whenever the state finds it useful to withdraw it, without prior warning, in a given case. "When you speak quietly at a private gathering," says the state, "you may say anything you please about the wisdom of a government policy *unless* a court later determines that interfering with your right at the time was more conducive to the public interest than protecting it." Such a right begins to resemble a so-called prima-facie right in that its exceptive clause is virtually unspecified and unlimited. It is only a small parody to interpret the prima-facie right as permission to do anything except what one shouldn't, and to interpret the nonabsolute "right" as permission to do anything for which permission is not subsequently withdrawn. These are hardly "rights" that one can stand upon, demand, fight for, or treasure. They are "rights" that make men humble, not claims that make men bold.

CHAPTER SIX

Human Rights

1. MORAL RIGHTS Legal and institutional rights are typically conferred by specific rules recorded in handbooks of regulations that can be observed and studied by the citizens or members subject to the rules. But not all rights are derived from such clearly visible laws and institutional regulations. On many occasions we assert that someone has a right to something even though we know there are no regulations or laws conferring such a right. Such talk clearly makes sense, so any theory of the nature of rights that cannot account for it is radically defective.

The term "moral rights" can be applied to all rights that are held to exist prior to, or independently of, any legal or institutional rules. Moral rights so conceived form a genus divisible into various species of rights having little in common except that they are not (necessarily) legal or institutional. The following are the main specific senses of "moral right": (1) A *conventional right* is one derived from established customs and expectations, whether or not recognized by law (e.g., an old woman's right to a young man's seat on a subway train). (2) An *ideal right* is not necessarily an actual right of any kind, but is rather what *ought* to be a positive (institutional or conventional) right, and would be so in a better or ideal legal system or conventional code. (3) A *conscientious right* is a claim the recognition of which as valid is called for, not (necessarily) by actual or ideal rules or conventions, but rather by the principles of an enlightened individual conscience. (4) An *exercise right* is not, strictly speaking, a right at all, though it is so-called in popular usage; it is simply moral justification in the exercise of a right of some other kind, the latter right remaining in one's possession and unaffected by considerations bearing on the rightness or wrongness of its exercising. When a person speaks of a moral right, he may be referring to a generically moral right not further specified, or to a right in one of these four specific senses; sometimes the context does not reveal which sense of "moral" is employed, and the possibility of equivocation is always present.

2. HUMAN RIGHTS

Among the rights that are commonly said to be moral in the generic sense (that is, independent of legal or other institutional recognition) are some also called "human rights." Human rights are sometimes understood to be ideal rights, sometimes conscientious rights, and sometimes both. In any case, they are held to be closely associated with actual claims. If a given human right is an ideal right, then human rightholders do or will have a claim against political legislators to convert (eventually) their "moral right" into a positive legal one. If the human right in question is a conscientious right, then it is an actual claim against private individuals for a certain kind of treatment—a claim that holds *now*, whatever the positive law may say about it.

I shall define "human rights" to be generically moral rights of a fundamentally important kind held equally by all human beings, unconditionally and unalterably. Whether these rights are "moral" in any of the more precise senses, I shall leave an open question to be settled by argument, not definition. Of course, it is also an open question whether there *are* any human rights and, if so, just what those rights are. All of the rights that have been characterized as "natural rights" in the leading manifestoes[1] can also be called human rights, but, as I shall be using the terms, not all human rights are also by definition natural rights. The theory of natural rights asserts not only that there are certain human rights, but also that these rights have certain further epistemic properties and a certain metaphysical status. In respect to questions of moral ontology and moral epistemology, the theory of human rights is neutral. Finally, it should be noticed that our definition includes the phrase "*all* human beings" but does not say "*only* human beings," so that a human right held by animals is not excluded by definition.

In addition to the characteristics mentioned in our definition, human

---

1 E.g., the American Declaration of Independence (1776), the Virginia Bill of Rights (1775), and the French Declaration of the Rights of Man and of Citizens (1789).

rights have also been said to be "absolute." Sometimes this is simply a redundancy, another way of referring to the properties of universality and inalienability; but sometimes "absoluteness" is meant to refer to an additional characteristic, which in turn is subject to at least three interpretations. Human rights can be absolute, first, only in the sense that all rights are absolute, namely, unconditionally incumbent within the limits of their well-defined scope. Second, a human right might be held to be absolute in the sense that the rights to life, liberty, and the pursuit of happiness, as proclaimed in the Declaration of Independence, are most plausibly interpreted as absolute, namely, as "ideal directives" to relevant parties to "do their best" for the values involved. If the state has seriously considered Doe's right to his land, done its best to find alternative routes for a public road, and compensated Doe as generously as possible before expropriating him by eminent domain, it has faithfully discharged its duty of "due consideration" that is the correlative of his "right to property" conceived simply as an ideal directive. If a human right is absolute only in the sense in which an ideal directive is absolute, then it is satisfied whenever it is given the serious and respectful consideration it always deserves, even when that consideration is followed by a reluctant invasion of its corresponding interest.

The strongest and most interesting sense of "absolute" attributed to rights is that of being "absolutely exceptionless" not only within a limited scope but throughout a scope *itself* unlimited. The right to free speech would be absolute in this sense *if* it protected all speech without exception in all circumstances. In that case, the limits of the right would correspond with the limit of the form of conduct specified, and once these wide boundaries had been defined, no further boundary adjustments, incursions or encumbrances, legislative restrictions, or conditions for emergency suspensions would be permitted. For a human right to have this character it would have to be such that no conflicts with other human rights, either of the same or another type, would be possible.

Some formulations of human rights might be passed off as absolute in the strongest sense merely because they are so vaguely put. Some are formulated in conditional language ("a right to adequate nutrition *if* or *when* food is available") and then held to be absolute qua conditional. Other rights, put in glittering and general language ("a right to be treated like a human being," "a right to be treated like a person, not a thing") are safely held to be absolute because without detailed specification they yield few clear and uncontroversial injunctions. Others are formulated in language containing "standard-bearing terms" such as "reasonable," "proper," or "worthy," without any clue to the standards to be employed in applying these terms. Thus it is said that all men (like all animals) have a right not to be treated cruelly. So far, so good; there can be no exceptions to that right. But its "absoluteness" can be seen to be merely formal when one considers that cruel treatment is treatment that inflicts *unnecessary, unreasonable,* or *improper* suffering on its victim. The air of self-evidence and security beyond all controversy immediately disappears from this human right when men come to propose and debate precise standards of necessity, reasonableness, and propriety.

We should not despair, however, of finding explicit standards of (say) cruelty that will give human rights content and yet leave them plausible candidates for absoluteness in the strong sense. The right not to be *tortured,* for example, comes close to exhaustive definability in nonstandard-bearing terms, and may be such that it cannot conflict with other rights, including other human rights, and can therefore be treated as categorical and exceptionless. If torture is still too vague a term, we can give exact empirical descriptions of the Chinese Water Torture, the Bamboo Fingernail Torture, and so on, and then claim that everyone has an absolutely exceptionless right in every conceivable circumstance not to be treated in any of those precisely described ways. Does this right pass the test of nonconflict with other rights?

Suppose a foreign tyrant of Caligulan character demands of our government that it seize certain political critics, imprison them, and slowly torture them to death, and threatens that unless that is done, his police will seize the members of our diplomatic staff in his country and torture *them* to death. At first sight this appears to be an authentic case of conflict between human rights, in that it would be impossible to do anything that would have as its consequence the fulfillment of everyone's right not to be tortured. What we should say about this blackmail situation if we wish to maintain that the right not to be tortured is nevertheless absolute (exceptionless and nonconflictable) is as follows. If the political critics in our grasp have a human right never to be tortured, then we have a categorical duty not to torture them. Thus, we ought not and will not torture them. We know, however, that this is likely to lead to the torture of the diplomatic hostages. We should therefore make every effort to dissuade Caligula, perhaps even through military pressure, not to carry out his threat. If Caligula nevertheless tortures his hostages, their rights have been infringed, but by Caligula, *not by us.*

All cases of apparent conflict of rights not to be tortured can be treated in this way. Whenever it is impossible to honor all of them, the situation causing that impossibility is itself the voluntary creation of human beings. Nothing in nature itself can ever bring such a conflict into existence. A tyrant's threat is in this respect unlike a plague that renders it impossible for everybody to get enough to eat. It would be idle to claim that the right to enough food is an absolute, categorial right, exceptionless in every conceivable circumstance, because we cannot legislate over nature. But we can legislate for man (the argument continues), and this is a plausible way to do it: *No acts of torture anywhere at any time are ever to be permitted.* All human beings can thus be possessed of a right that is absolutely exceptionless. That we have no guarantee that some people somewhere won't violate it or try to force us to violate it is no argument against the "legislation" itself.

There is therefore no objection in principle to the idea of human rights that are absolute in the sense of being categorically exceptionless. It is another question as to whether there are such rights, and what they might be. The most plausible candidates, like the right not to be tortured, will be passive negative rights, that is, rights not to be done to by others in certain ways. It is more difficult to think of active negative rights (rights not to be interfered with) or positive rights (rights to be done to in certain ways) as absolutely exceptionless. The positive rights to be given certain essentials —food, shelter, security, education—clearly depend upon the existence of an adequate supply, something that cannot be guaranteed categorically and universally.

If absoluteness in this strong sense is made part of the very meaning of the expression "human right," then it would seem that there is a lamentable paucity of human rights, if any at all. Clarity will best be served, I think, if we keep "absoluteness" out of the definition of "human right." Two questions can then be kept separate: (1) Are there any human rights, i.e., generically moral, unforfeitable, irrevocable rights held equally and universally by human beings (at least)? (2) If so, are any of these rights absolute? We turn now to a consideration of the grounds for thinking that there are human rights, so defined.

3. GROUNDS FOR EQUALITY   Despite its current popularity, the theory that there are rights held equally by all human beings continues to trouble philosophers. It is natural for them to imagine skeptics asking: "Why *all* human beings *equally,* and not only, or primarily, the deserving ones?" The skeptical question still has great force. To appreciate this we have only to consider that the theory of human rights requires that in certain basic ways we treat even congenital idiots and convicted mass murderers the same as everyone else.

To appreciate fully how revolutionary the idea of equal human rights was, recall how European society was organized during the centuries preceding the revolutionary period. The feudal system recognized distinct hereditary castes, each with its peculiar and irreducible legal status defined by elaborate sets of rights and duties. A legal *status* in the relevant sense differs from mere social roles like father, promiser, and farmer, in part because it is entirely hereditary and unmodifiable by voluntary arrangements. The rights men had as a matter of status were theirs as royalty, nobility, clergy, serfs, and so on; there was nothing "equal" about these status rights. Human rights, as a revolutionary idea, were associated with the idea of a single status society where the powers of the high and mighty were limited everywhere by the rights all persons derived from their "status" as human beings.

The single status society differs strikingly from a society with fixed hereditary caste distinctions as well as from a purely meritarian society in which *all* political rights are based on merit alone. Gregory Vlastos, in an important article,[2] has argued that the doctrine of universal equal human rights presupposes a concept of equal and universal human *worth* that is to be sharply distinguished from the idea of human merits. We grade persons according to their talents, skills, character and personality traits, and other rankable qualities, but in respect to "human worth" (by definition) all men must get equal grades. Indeed, "human worth," is not a "grading concept" at all. In this it differs from every kind of merit, including, of course, moral merit, in respect to which there are vast inequalities among persons. In a society based on human rights, at least some rights will belong irrevocably to fools and rogues as well as to everyone else. These are the rights, Vlastos suggests, that are based on the worth human beings have as individuals, quite apart from their valuable qualities.

Acknowledging another person's "human worth" is in one respect strikingly similar to (but by no means identical with) *loving* another person, for neither is dependent on the grades we give to the other person's merits. "Constancy of affection in the face of variations of merit is one of the surest tests of whether a parent does love a child."[3] A parent may admire one child more than another, or like (in the sense of enjoy) one more than another, or judge one higher than another; but it is a necessary condition of parental love that it not fluctuate with these responses to merit. Love is a response to a person as an individual, not as a dispensible possessor of meritorious qualities.

In ordinary life, at least where the idea of human rights is a commonplace, the notion of human worth transfers easily to strangers whom we in no sense love. "If I see a stranger in danger of drowning," writes Vlastos, "I am not likely to ask myself questions about his moral character before going to his aid. . . . My obligation here is to a man, to any man in such circumstances, not to a good man."[4] The familiarity of this example indicates that we attach a value ("worth") to any human life, no matter what the conceivable character of its possessor. Since this is a response to value wholly independent of perceived qualities, it is by definition a response to what Vlastos calls "human worth." There are many such examples:

[2] Gregory Vlastos, "Justice and Equality," in *Social Justice*, ed. Richard B. Brandt (Englewood Cliffs, N.J.: Prentice-Hall, Inc., 1962), pp. 31–72.

[3] Vlastos, "Justice and Equality," p. 44.

[4] Vlastos, "Justice and Equality," p. 47.

To be sincere, reliable, fair, kind, tolerant, unintrusive, modest in my relations with my fellows is not due them because they have made brilliant or even passing moral grades, but simply because they happen to be members of the moral community. It is not necessary to add "members in good standing": the moral community is not a club from which members may be dropped for delinquency. Our morality does not provide for moral outcastes or half-castes. It does provide for punishment. But this takes place *within* the moral community and under its rules. It is for this reason that, for example, one has no right to be cruel to a cruel person. His offense against the moral law has not put him outside the law. He is still protected by its prohibition of cruelty—as much so as are kind persons. The pain inflicted on him as punishment for his offense does not close out the great reserve of good will on the part of others which is his birthright as a human being; it is a limited withdrawal from it. Capital punishment even is no exception. The fact that a man has been condemned to death does not license his jailors to beat him or virtuous citizens to lynch him.[5]

A society based on human rights is actually closer to the old fixed status idea (except that it has but a single status) than to the society in which all basic rights are distributed in proportion to merit. *Some* rights in any society, of course, will have to be based on merit, but the ones that are independent of merit define the class in which human rights are located.

Why treat all people equally in any respect in the face of manifest inequalities of merit among them? The skeptic's challenge has not been met, and is certainly not disposed of by the reply that all humans are equal in "moral worth," whatever their other differences. No skeptic who denies equal rights will be easily convinced that there is equal human worth. Whatever kind of value "human worth" may be, if it is generically like every other kind of worth it is a *supervenient* property,[6] i.e., a property possessed by something in virtue of some other property or properties it possesses. It is impossible that two things should be alike in every other respect and have different degrees of worth, for degree of worth is determined by other characteristics. If one is more worthy than the other it must be *because* they have different properties. Similarly, if two things or two persons have the same worth (any kind of worth), they must have in common some other characteristic—a nonvalue characteristic—that is the basis of their equal worth. But what might this common characteristic be? Philosophical champions of human rights have replied to this legitimate query with a bewildering variety of answers, almost all of them inadequate.

Most philosophers agree with their skeptical challengers that if there are certain rights possessed by all men independently of their merits, this must be because, despite their many inequalities, all men are equal in some one respect that is of supreme moral importance. In attempting to identify this respect, some mention other *value characteristics;* some opt for certain

[5] Vlastos, "Justice and Equality," p. 47.
[6] R. M. Hare, *The Language of Morals* (Oxford: Oxford University Press, 1952), pp. 80 ff.

natural capacities, no matter how fully realized, such as "rationality," or for *natural vulnerabilities,* such as the liability to pain and suffering; others leave the empirical world altogether in search of *transcendental properties,* an intrinsic dignity attaching to all human beings as "ends in themselves."

None of this has proved very satisfactory. The intrinsically moral qualities invoked to explain equal human worth must rest, as moral qualities, on some common nonvalue characteristics which are *their* bases or determinants; the question about the nature of the common characteristic arises all over again about them. If human beings have human worth *because* of their "intrinsic pricelessness" or "infinite value," asks the skeptic, where do those extravagantly dimensioned endowments come from? In virtue of what other traits can *they* be properly ascribed? These questions seem even more appropriate and difficult to answer than the question that was their occasion. Worse still, the "moral property" approach often involves, in the words of A. I. Melden, "the radical muddle that if one could somehow see...into the very depths of a person's being, one would somehow find a quality of sheer preciousness in itself that endows a person with his status as the possessor of a right."[7] Part of the muddle consists in treating the mysterious value property "preciousness" as if it were not supervenient upon other characteristics, and hence not a genuine value characteristic at all. Surely to "see" a person as precious is to see him *as he is* and *therefore* precious. It is not to see the preciousness directly, as one might see a dab of paint on a wall. Preciousness is not "a kind of mystic moral badge" worn on the wall of the soul; it is a way of valuing something based on an awareness of the kind of thing it is.

Empirical characteristics, especially natural capabilities and vulnerabilities, are somewhat more plausible candidates for grounds of human worth, since their candidacies do not involve regresses or logical muddles. But very little more than that can be said for them. The capability most commonly favored for this role is man's unique *rationality.* Some men are more rational than others, however, and we do not want it to follow that the more rational are the more worthy, for that would be to make variable merit a ground for invariant worth. It might be said that all men, even the most irrational, have the potential to be rational, but again it would seem that even these universal potentials are unequal. Perhaps what is meant is that all men have the potential to be at least minimally rational, that is, to measure up to a modest standard that exceeds anything lower animals can reach. That may be true in some extremely weak sense of "potential" (in which even an irreparably brain-damaged idiot still has the "potential" to be rational), but it is difficult to discern any intuitive connection between such weak potentiality and human worth. In more familiar senses of "potential," many possessors of human rights are not even potentially rational.

7 A. I. Melden, *Rights and Right Conduct* (Oxford: Basil Blackwell, 1959), p. 80.

The natural vulnerability most commonly favored as a ground of human worth is liability to pain and suffering. This criterion would also permit entry of lower animals into the moral community, but we needn't cavil over that. It does have difficulties of a more serious kind. Some of these stem from the fact that liabilities to pain and suffering can vary from person to person. Some people are naturally more sensitive than others; does this make them more worthy? Moreover, drugs and other artificial devices might be used to accentuate these natural differences. The most serious difficulty, however, is that certain forms of treatment presumably violative of human rights might cause no pain or suffering at all, such as the sudden painless murder of an innocent man who has no family or friends to grieve for him.

Various terms from the metaphysical vocabulary "explain" human worth only by renaming that which is to be explained. Thus, without further explanation, the fact that all human beings are "persons, not things" or the claim that "men are ends in themselves" do not clearly account for the equality of human worth. Similarly, that men are "sacred" or of "infinite value"[8] are other (and perhaps better) ways of putting the claim of equal worth, but not descriptions of the grounds of that worth. If "sacred" (like "precious") is best defined as being the proper object of a certain kind of attitude, then the fact of a man's sacredness cannot be invoked in justification of that attitude without a kind of trivializing circularity. It would be like telling a man he ought to be amused by a joke, and then justifying that claim by asserting that the joke is amusing. That would give the unamused no insight into the basis of the joke he is unable to appreciate, and leave his "skepticism" untouched. Finally, it will not do, for similar reasons, to rest the case for equal and universal human worth on "our common humanity," for we wish to know precisely what it is about our common humanity that makes it so worthy of our respect.

[8] The metaphor of infinitude has its point. An infinite set is defined as one that contains a proper subset such that there is a one-to-one correspondence between the members of the set and those of its own subset. Thus, the class of all cardinal integers is infinite since it contains a proper subset (the class of all odd numbers) that has as many members as it does! In transfinite arithmetic, the (infinite) number of all cardinal numbers is called "aleph-null" (after the Hebrew letter), and it can be shown that aleph-null plus any finite number equals aleph-null; aleph-null minus any finite number equals aleph-null; aleph-null plus or times itself, or taken to any finite power of itself, still equals aleph-null! Hence the laws of transfinite arithmetic are quite different from those of ordinary arithmetic. This should sober the hasty "rationalists" in politics who would murder finite numbers of human beings for the sake of many millions of other human beings, including those unborn. If *each* life is of "infinite" value, that kind of political arithmetic doesn't work, as each life is the equal of all the others combined. For a simple statement of the basic notions of transfinite arithmetic presupposing no more mathematics than elementary arithmetic, see Edward Kasner and James Newman, *Mathematics and the Imagination* (New York: Simon and Schuster, Inc., 1940), Chap. II. For a perceptive critique of the misuse of "moral arithmetic" in Stalinist Russia, see Arthur Koestler, *Darkness at Noon* (New York: The Macmillan Company, 1941).

It may well be that universal "respect" for human beings is, in a sense, "groundless"—a kind of ultimate attitude not itself justifiable in more ultimate terms. This is what might be said, after all, about parental (and other) love. The parent's unshaken love for the child who has gone bad may not be a response to any merit of the child (he may have none), or to any of his observable qualities (he may be a repulsive brute). In such a case, no quality of the child can be cited as a "reason" in justification of the parent's love. "I am his father after all" might be said to *explain* to others an affection that might otherwise seem wholly unintelligible, but that does not state a *ground* for the affection so much as indicate that it is "groundless" (but not irrational or mysterious for that). The "respect" said by Kant and many others to be owed to every human being by his fellows is not the same as affection or love, but it may well share this logical feature of ultimacy and "groundlessness" with it.

We are generally not puzzled by the fact that parents can love their children in a "groundless" and ultimate way, because we assume that normal human beings are equipped by their biological natures with the disposition to react in just that way to their own children. Respect for the human worth of strangers and villains, however, is a more mysterious phenomenon. It may well be, however, that most normal people are disposed to fall into that attitude whenever their attention is drawn to certain traits of all humans, or when they acquire the habit of looking at (or conceiving) their fellows in a certain way. The traits thus attended to may not constitute logically coercive reasons in support of the attitude of Kantian respect (that may be too much to hope for), but a thorough awareness of them can make the attitude seem less mysterious and actually lead people to acquire it— a result almost as good! We can think of our fellows simply as wise or entertaining, threatening or helpful, sexually attractive, authorities, physicians, or cooks, and adopt the attitude appropriate to the category. Bernard Williams contrasts these narrowly personal or technical attitudes toward another with what he calls the "human point of view," which is "concerned primarily with what it is for *him* to live that life and do those actions in that character."[9] When we look at a person from that perspective, we do not simply regard him as "the surface to which a certain label can be applied"; rather we "try to see the world (including the label) from *his* point of view."[10] The real point of the maxim that all men are equal may be simply that all men equally have a point of view of their own, a unique angle from which they view the world. They are all equally centers of experience, foci of subjectivity. This implies that they are all capable of

9 Bernard Williams, "The Idea of Equality," in *Philosophy, Politics, and Society* (second series), ed. P. Laslett and W. G. Runciman (New York: Barnes & Noble, Inc., 1962), p. 115.
10 Williams, "The Idea of Equality," p. 116.

being viewed by others imaginatively from their own point of view. They "have shoes" into which we can always try to put ourselves; this is not true of mere things. It may follow (causally, not logically) from this way of so regarding them that we come to *respect* them in the sense tied to the idea of "human worth."

"Human worth" itself is best understood to name no property in the way that "strength" names strength and "redness" redness. In attributing human worth to everyone we may be ascribing no property or set of qualities, but rather expressing an attitude—the attitude of respect—toward the humanity in each man's person. That attitude follows naturally from regarding everyone from the "human point of view," but it is not grounded on anything more ultimate than itself, and it is not demonstrably justifiable.

It can be argued further against skeptics that a world with equal human rights is a *more just* world, a way of organizing society for which we would all opt if we were designing our institutions afresh in ignorance of the roles we might one day have to play in them. It is also a *less dangerous* world generally, and one with a *more elevated and civilized* tone. If none of this convinces the skeptic, we should turn our backs on him to examine more important problems.

4. ABSOLUTE AND NONABSOLUTE HUMAN RIGHTS

In December 1948, the General Assembly of the United Nations adopted a Universal Declaration of Human Rights. Unlike the eighteenth-century manifestoes of natural rights, which were concerned almost exclusively with the individual's rights not to be interfered with by others, the U.N. Declaration endorses numerous basic positive rights to receive benefits and be provided with the means to satisfy basic human needs. Even the conception in the U.N. document of a basic need (in contrast to an unneeded but valuable commodity) reflected changes in the world's outlook and hopes since the eighteenth century. The U.N. Declaration contains the old-style negative rights, mostly pertaining to civic and political activities and criminal procedures, as well as the new "social and economic rights" that are correlated with the positive duties of others (usually of the state). Rights of the former kind impose duties upon private citizens and the state alike to keep hands off individuals in certain respects, to leave them alone.

Other articles, however, impose duties upon others that are so difficult that they may, under widely prevalent conditions of scarcity and conflict, be impossible for *anyone* to discharge. Articles 22–27, for example, state that "everyone, as a member of society...has the right to work, to free choice of employment...to protection against unemployment...to just and favorable remuneration...to rest and leisure...and periodic holidays with pay ...to food, clothing, housing, and medical care...to education...to enjoy the arts and to share in scientific advancement and its benefits."[11] Now, as we have seen,[12] these positive (as opposed to negative) human rights are rights in an unusual new "manifesto sense," for, unlike all other claim-rights, they are not necessarily correlated with the duties of any assignable persons. The Declaration must therefore be interpreted to say that all men as such have a claim (that is, are in a position to make claim) to the goods therein mentioned, even if there should temporarily be no one in the corresponding position to be claimed against.

These social and economic human rights, therefore, are certainly not *absolute* rights, since easily imaginable and commonly actual circumstances can reduce them to mere claims. Moreover, these rights are clearly not nonconflictable. For example, where there are two persons for every job, there must be conflict between the claims of some workers to "free choice of employment," in the sense that if one worker's claim is recognized as valid, another's *must* be rejected.

Can any human rights plausibly be construed as absolutely exceptionless and therefore nonconflictable in principle, or must all rights in their very natures be vulnerable to legitimate invasion in some circumstances? The most plausible candidates for absoluteness are (some) *negative rights;* since they require no positive actions or contributions from others, they are less likely to be affected by conditions of scarcity. To say of a given negative right that it is nonconflictable is to say: (1) if conflicts occur with rights of other kinds, it must always win, and (2) no conflict is possible with other rights of its own kind. The right to speak freely is a plausible human right and is conferred by Article 19 of the U.N. Declaration, but it is certainly not nonconflictable in the sense defined above, for it cannot plausibly be said always and necessarily to win out whenever it conflicts with another's right to reputation, privacy, or safety. In theory, of course, we could consistently hold that the free expression right always overrides rights of other kinds, but then that right would fail to satisfy the second condition for non-conflictability, no matter how stubbornly we back it. The requirement that the right in question be incapable in principle of conflicting with another person's right of the *same* kind is the real stumbling block in the path of absoluteness. Consider an audience of hecklers exercising *their* "free speech" to shout down a speaker, or some scoundrel using his "free speech" to persuade others to cut out the tongue of his hated rival. In these cases, free speech must be limited in its *own* interest. Similar examples can be provided, *mutatis mutandis,* for freedom of movement, free exercise of religion, the right to property, and to virtually all of the characteristically eighteenth-century rights of noninterference.

11 UNESCO, *Human Rights, a symposium* (London and New York: Allan Wingate, 1949).
12 *Supra,* pp. 66 f.

There remain at least three kinds of human rights that may very well be understood (without obvious absurdity) to be absolute and nonconflictable. Positive rights to "goods" that cannot ever, in the very nature of the case, be in scarce supply, are one possibility. Perhaps the right to a fair trial (really a package of positive and negative rights) or the right to equal protection of the law,[13] or "the right to equal consideration,"[14] fall into this category.

A second possibility is the negative right not to be treated inhumanely or cruelly, not to be tortured or treated barbarously.[15] Whether we as legislators (actual or ideal) should confer such an absolute right on everyone is entirely up to us. There may be good policy reasons against it, but if we are convinced by the powerful policy and moral reasons in favor of it, we needn't be deterred by the fear of conflictability. As I argued in the previous section, we can *decide* without absurdity to let this right override rights of all *other* kinds, and there is nothing in nature to bring this right into conflict with other persons' rights of the *same* kind. Article 5 of the U.N. Declaration, which forbids "torture or...cruel, inhuman...treatment," may be conceived as conferring a human right in a very strong sense, namely one which is not only universal and inalienable, but also absolute. It is still not a human right in the very strongest sense—one that applies absolutely and unalterably to all and *only* humans—for it is presumably the one right that the higher animals have, if they have any rights at all.

A third possibility is the right not to be subjected to exploitation or degradation even when such subjection is utterly painless and therefore not cruel. It is possible to treat human beings with drugs, hypnosis, or other brainwashing techniques so that they become compliant tools in the hands of their manipulators, useful as means to their manipulators' ends, but with all serious purposes of their own totally obliterated. Once human beings are in this condition, they may have no notion that they are being exploited or degraded, having come to accept and internalize their exploiters' image of themselves as their own. In this state, human beings might be raised, as Swift suggested, for food, fattened up for a few years, and then slaughtered (humanely, of course); or they might be harnessed, like donkeys, to wagons or millstones. It would be good business as well as good morals to treat them kindly (so long as they are obedient), for that way one can get more labor out of them in the long run. Clearly, kindness and "humanity," while sufficient to satisfy the rights of animals, are not sufficient for human beings,

---

[13] As suggested by L. B. Frantz. Cf. *supra*, p. 81.

[14] "Notice...that there is one ['natural'] right which...is to all intents and purposes an absolute right. That is the right to equal consideration—the right to be treated as the formula for justice provides. For this right is one which is the most basic of all, one which is under no conditions to be violated." Lucius Garvin, *A Modern Introduction to Ethics* (Boston: Houghton Mifflin Company, 1953), p. 491.

[15] See *supra*, pp. 86–88.

who must therefore have ascribed to them another kind of right that we deliberately withhold from animals. That is a right to a higher kind of respect, an inviolate dignity, which as a broad category includes the negative rights not to be brainwashed, not to be made into a docile instrument for the purposes of others, and not to be converted into a domesticated animal. Rights in this category are probably the only ones that are human rights in the strongest sense: unalterable, "absolute" (exceptionless and noncon-flictable), and universally and *peculiarly* human.

CHAPTER SEVEN

Social

Justice

1. COMPARATIVE AND NONCOMPARATIVE JUSTICE The problems of justice of most direct concern to social theory are those that necessarily involve comparisons of the claims of more than one person, and require that some sort of balance be struck between them. Occasions for these interpersonal comparisons do not by any means exhaust all the occasions of justice. In some contexts, an individual's rights or deserts alone determine what is due him, and once we have come to a judgment of his due, that judgment cannot be logically affected by subsequent knowledge of the condition of other parties. When our task is to do noncomparative justice (as we might call it) to each of a large number of individuals, we do not compare them with each other, but rather compare each in turn with an objective standard and judge each "on his own merits." Equality of treatment, therefore, is no part of the concept of noncomparative (individual) justice, even though it is a central element in comparative (social) justice. If we treat *everybody* unfairly by the relevant noncomparative standard, but equally and impartially so, we have done an injustice to each that is barely mitigated by the equal injustice done all the others.[1]

[1] Cf. the sports column of *Newsweek,* Sept. 14, 1970, p. 123, in which the toughness of the late professional football coach, Vincent Lombardi, is discussed: "Tackle Henry Jordan's oft-quoted remark indicated the fairness of the coach: 'He treated us all the same. Like dogs.' "

Our concern in this chapter will be with judgments of fairness that are essentially comparative. The main occasions for social or comparative justice are: the allocation of burdens and benefits, the legislation and administration of general rules, and the voluntary coming together in cooperative undertakings, or in games and other competitive activities. Comparative injustice under all these headings consists in the creation or modification of a *relation* between parties: unfair discrimination, arbitrary exclusion, favoritism, inappropriate partisanship or partiality, inconsistent rule-enforcement, "freeloading" in a cooperative undertaking, or putting one party at a relative disadvantage in a competition.

2. FORMAL AND MATERIAL PRINCIPLES The basic principle of comparative justice is that like cases are to be treated alike and different cases to be treated differently. If Doe gets a large share and Roe a small share in a distribution, our sense of justice is not satisfied until we learn of some respect in which Doe and Roe differ that underlies and justifies this difference in treatment. If Doe and Roe are exactly alike in every respect, but one is given more than the other, the discrimination in their treatment is totally arbitrary, and *arbitrary discrimination* is the essence of comparative injustice. Indeed, many writers[2] hold that the principle of like treatment for like cases is more than simply one among many ethical principles vying for our allegiance, but is rather an instance of a more general principle that is constitutive of *rationality* itself. One would violate this more general principle by ascribing different geometrical properties to two identical isosceles triangles, or by holding that a given physical event was a lonely exception to Newton's Laws, as much as by denying equal protection of the law to those citizens who have black skins.

Any two persons or things will differ in *some* respects, and it is always possible to cite some difference between them in support (more precisely, in *justicization*)[3] of differences in the way they are treated. Clearly, then, comparative justice requires more than that difference in treatment be based on differences in characteristics. The underlying differences between individuals that justicize differences in their treatment must be *relevant* differences, and the underlying similarities that justicize similar treatment

---

2 E.g., Isaiah Berlin, "Equality As An Ideal," *Proceedings of the Aristotelian Society,* LVI (1955–56); Chaim Perelman, *The Idea of Justice and the Problem of Argument* (New York: Humanities Press, Inc., 1963), pp. 1–60.

3 I borrow this useful term from W. K. Frankena, "The Concept of Social Justice," in *Social Justice,* ed. R. B. Brandt (Englewood Cliffs, N.J.: Prentice-Hall, Inc., 1961), p. 5, and A. D. Woozley, "Injustice," *American Philosophical Quarterly Monograph,* 7 (1973). To *justify* an act is to show that it is on balance and in the last analysis, all things considered, *right*. To *justicize* an act is to show only that it is *just,* and therefore tends to be right. Since (as we have seen) not all just acts are right, and not all right acts are just, the distinction between justicization and on-balance justification is useful.

must be *relevant* similarities. Injustice is done when individuals who are alike in every relevant respect (not in absolutely every respect) are treated differently, or when individuals who are different in some relevant respect are treated alike.

The principle of like treatment, then, is only a starting place in the analysis of comparative justice, and needs supplementation by criteria for determining the relevance of differences. For that reason, the like treatment principle is usually said to be merely a *formal principle of justice,* and the criteria of relevance for various contexts of justice with which it must be supplemented are called *material principles of justice.*[4] A formal principle of justice, in the words of a recent writer on the subject, "contains a completely unspecified variable whereas material principles constitute different ways of replacing the variable by a constant."[5] The principle that persons who are alike in the relevant respects must be treated alike, while persons who are unalike in the relevant respects must be treated unalike and in direct proportion to the differences between them is formal in the defined sense, since it fails completely to specify which respects are relevant. The principle that social wealth should be distributed to each in proportion to his contribution (or, alternately, his ability, need, rank, or virtue) is a material principle, since it at least goes a long way toward specifying which characteristics are relevant to the justice of distributions of social wealth.

The principle that like cases should be treated alike is put too hastily by some equalitarian writers in the form of a "presumption for equality." It is commonly said, for example, that although it is absurd to think that justice requires us to treat all men exactly alike, it does require that we give them equal treatment until we have good reason not to do so, that "the burden of proof is on the person who wants to treat people differently from one another...."[6] But this presumptive principle is by no means identical in meaning or implications to the formal principle as we have formulated it. Our formal principle (which derives from Aristotle) would have us: (1) treat alike (equally) those who are the same (equal) in relevant respects, and (2) treat unalike (unequally) those who are unalike (unequal) in relevant respects, in direct proportion to the differences (inequalities) between them. The equalitarian presumptivist formulation completely ignores the second part of this principle in insisting that all and only departures from *equal* treatment need justification. Clearly, what needs justification

---

[4] The best explication I know of the distinction between formal and material principles of justice is that of Louis I. Katzner, "An Analysis of the Concept of Justice" (Ph.D. dissertation, University of Michigan, 1968). I am heavily indebted to that excellent work in the paragraphs that follow.

[5] Katzner, "An Analysis of the Concept of Justice," p. 2.

[6] Katzner, "An Analysis of the Concept of Justice," p. 37, paraphrasing S. Benn and R. S. Peters, *Social Principles and the Democratic State* (London: George Allen and Unwin Ltd., 1959), p. 111.

according to the double formula above are: (1) departures from identical (equal) treatment when individuals seem to be the same (equal) in relevant respects, *and* (2) departures from different (unequal) treatment when individuals seem to be different (unequal) in relevant respects. Where the "burden of proof" actually lies in a given case, then, depends upon what is given (believed or known) about the relevant traits of the individuals involved, and also upon the particular context of justice and its governing norms and maxims. The presumption in favor of equal treatment holds when the individuals involved are believed, assumed, or expected to be equal in the relevant respects, whereas the presumption in favor of *unequal* treatment holds when the individuals involved are expected to be different in the relevant respects.

Consider some examples. If two pupils both violate the same rule but one is given a more severe penalty, we would *presume* (knowing no more facts) that a comparative injustice had been committed by the teacher. Unless some relevant difference between the two offenders or their offenses could be brought to light by the teacher, we would treat the presumption as decisive. On the other hand, consider the example cited by Louis Katzner to show that sometimes the "burden of proof" is on those who advocate equality of treatment. A testator whose sole survivor is his son leaves one half of his estate to that son and, "equally," one half to another person of the son's age. The two inheritors are different in a respect we normally take to be relevant in such contexts, namely that one is a member of the testator's immediate family whereas the other is not. Because of this *given* relevant difference, the father has the burden of presenting a justification for *treating two people equally* that will override the presumption that they should be treated differently.

The equalitarian presumptivist principle, then, errs in overlooking cases in which our antecedent expectations about the existence of characteristics agreed to be relevant creates a presumption in favor of inequality. The disguised normative character of the principle ("disguised" when it is claimed to be the formal principle of comparative justice), and, more importantly, its ultimately arbitrary character, are shown by a consideration of how it would apply to cases where no expectation exists about the equal or unequal degree to which relevant characteristics are possessed by those subject to our treatment. The presumptive principle, in these cases, tells us to presume even in our ignorance that equal treatment is called for, that individuals about whom we know nothing should nevertheless be treated equally unless or until grounds for distinction between them can be found. In this instance, the presumptive principle clearly reveals itself as not "merely formal"; it purports to be a decisive guide to our conduct. Thus, a controversial (and indeed very doubtful!) normative principle is presented in the guise of a purely formal principle of reason supposedly definitive of the very nature of comparative justice. The moral of the story is this: Don't confuse an *exceptive principle* ("Treat all men alike *except* where there are relevant differences between them") with a *presumptive principle* ("Treat all men alike *until it can be shown* that there are relevant differences between them"). The exceptive principle is indeed formal, providing no guide to action or grounds for presuming either equality or inequality in the case in which we are ignorant of the characteristics of the men to be treated. The presumptive principle has us presume equal treatment even in this case, and that would be to make a presumption every bit as arbitrary as the presumption in favor of *unequal* treatment in the absence of knowledge of the relevant similarities and differences of the persons involved.

Stating the correct principles of *material justice* (criteria of relevance) is a task of a different order from that involved in formulating the principle of formal justice. Deciding which material principles to adopt requires us to enter the moral arena itself, where basic attitudes are in profound opposition, and social interests and political parties contend. The issues involved here, being substantive moral questions rather than questions of conceptual analysis with no direct normative implications, cannot be settled decisively by appeals to "the very definition of the concept of justice." We shall have to bring in normative principles from the outside so that justice can have substance and provide direction.

The choice of material principles is sometimes severely limited by the context itself, and is therefore not particularly difficult or controversial. We should not discriminate between persons who are alike in all relevant respects; but which respects are relevant depends upon the occasion for justice, on our purposes and objectives, and on the internal rules of the "game" we are playing. There is no one kind of characteristic that is relevant in all contexts, no single material principle that applies universally. In short, what we seek when we look for a material principle is what H. L. A. Hart has called "a shifting or varying criterion used in determining when, *for any given purpose,* cases are alike or different."[7] Hart went on to make the interesting suggestion that there is an analogy between relevance to a given purpose and other relational notions: "In this respect, justice is like the notions of what is genuine [real], or tall, or warm, which contain an implicit reference to a standard which varies with the classification of the thing to which they are applied."[8] Thus, the standard of tallness varies depending on whether we are speaking of children, men, women, buildings, or mountains. There is no vicious "relativism" in this variation, and no skeptical affront to reason. It is useful to have words whose criteria of application vary in understood ways with the context, and "relevant" (as it occurs in formulations of the formal principle of comparative justice) is such a word.

[7] H. L. A. Hart, *The Concept of Law* (Oxford: The Clarendon Press, 1961), p. 156 (emphasis added).

[8] Hart, *The Concept of Law,* p. 156.

3. PRIZES Let us consider briefly three typical sorts of context in which questions of comparative justice arise: awards of prizes, administration and legislation of rules, and distributions of benefits and burdens. There is seldom any difficulty in deciding what is relevant when our business is to award a prize, or to judge the fairness of an award already made. If we have a clear idea in advance of what the prize is to be awarded *for,* we have a clear idea of which aspects of the various contestants are relevant. If we are awarding a prize for beauty, then physiognomy and bust, waist, and hip measurements are relevant, and IQ and swimming ability are not. If we are awarding a prize for distinguished work in physics, then the profundity, subtlety, and utility of a scientific discovery are relevant, but physiognomy and bust measurements are not. Surely *those* judgments of relevance and irrelevance are beyond controversy!

Sometimes rules govern the awards in a manner that gives judges no discretion. If we are awarding a prize for winning the one hundred yard dash, we must give it to the runner who crosses the finish line first after having obeyed all the rules along the way; the fact that another runner has a better previous record, or better form, or poorer luck, are totally "irrelevant." In other cases judges have room for interpretation, and must consider the purpose of the competition. To be sure, the "purpose" of an award, or notion of what the prize is for, is often obscure. Sometimes these matters are spelled out in detailed rules which may suffer from any of the flaws to which rules are prone: vagueness, ambiguity, inconsistency, incompleteness. It is especially common for the rules to entail the relevance of a plurality of characteristics and then give no guide as to how these incommensurables are to be weighted in importance. (Rulemakers *can* give such guidance by inventing arbitrary "point systems," like those which govern the judging of track, swimming, or gymnastic contests; often the rules do not even give that kind of guidance, as, for example, in the annual "Mother of the Year" awards.) But even when there are difficulties of these kinds in deciding how to award a prize, they are not typically confusions over *which* characteristics are relevant, but rather over relative weights attached to factors agreed to be relevant.

4. GENERAL RULES Consider next the context of rule administration. Enforcement of the law is unjust when it is irregular, random, or discriminatory, that is, when it is administered *unequally* among those to whom it applies. "If a rule forbids parking in a certain area," writes A. M. Honoré, "it is unfair to *A* who has parked in that area that he should be fined for doing so, whilst *B,* who has done the same thing, is not prosecuted."[9] (The unfairness in question is only comparative, since when

9 A. M. Honoré, "Social Justice," *McGill Law Journal,* Vol. 8 (1962), reprinted in *Essays in Legal Philosophy,* ed. Robert S. Summers (Berkeley and Los Angeles: University of California Press, 1968), p. 67.

A's case is considered on its own merits *exclusively,* and his "due" determined with no reference to the treatment of other parties, it will be manifest that he *has* received the treatment he deserves.) Similarly, if no one is permitted by a governing rule to cross the police lines in a demonstration area, it is unfair if the civilian brother-in-law of the police chief is allowed through.

General rules, however, almost always contain either express or implicit exceptive clauses defining more narrowly the class of persons to whom they apply, and the limiting conditions under which they cease to apply even to persons in that class. Authoritative orders and rules of law typically apply to *all* citizens *except* those of certain named classes who are, under specified conditions, granted exemptions or privileges denied to all others. Thus, *all* citizens must stay behind police lines (an order might say) *except* licensed journalists, Red Cross first aid teams, members of the Mayor's staff, and all members of the police force on active duty. Similarly, *all* motor vehicles must be driven through a residential area at thirty miles per hour or less *except* ambulances, fire engines, police cars on active service, or private cars in some extreme emergency. These exceptions, being recognized by the law itself, are by no means arbitrary, and a policeman who permits a journalist to cross a line or an ambulance to exceed the general speed limit is not committing an injustice to anyone. The police are not permitting "violations" of law, for the exceptive clauses are part of the very law the police and courts are sworn to enforce and to apply *equally* to everyone. Persons who are *relevantly* different must be treated differently, and the relevance of a given difference is determined by the law itself.

It is otherwise in the context of lawmaking, for the legislator must draw *his* notions of relevance from some source outside the law if he is to apply them in the formulation of new bills of legislation. Legislatures can make mistakes, or fall short of objectivity and impartiality in making the laws, with the result that some statutes are themselves unfair, granting undeserved privileges to whole *classes* of persons and arbitrarily withholding rights from other classes. A law permitting only white men access to National Parks would be arbitrarily discriminatory, basing a distinction upon a difference that is clearly irrelevant from the point of view of justice. Yet such a law could be enforced with perfect impartiality by the police and the courts. Hence, the justice or injustice of law administration is independent of the substantive justice or injustice of the laws themselves; just laws can be unfairly administered, and unjust laws administered with immaculate impartiality. Moreover, the comparative justice or injustice of the law is not determined by its conformity to (other) law, but by the relevance or irrelevance, as determined by independent standards, of the respects that are made the basis of discriminations in the law. General rules are unfair when they discriminate between classes that are actually alike in a respect that is "really and truly" relevant, and fail to discriminate between classes that are actually different in a respect that is "really and truly" relevant.

(Laws are subject to adverse criticism on many grounds other than injustice. They may be nondiscriminatory, but also inhumane, unnecessarily repressive, uneconomical, unenforcible, or foolish. But insofar as the criticism of law applies standards of comparative justice, it is aimed solely at discriminations between various classes of persons.)

Disagreements over the justice of laws (as opposed to the fairness of their administration) often seem to presuppose ultimate differences in values, but even here, genuine difficulty and controversy are more the exception than the rule. Why, for example, is the granting of a privilege to ambulance drivers to exceed posted speed limits not arbitrary, whereas the same privilege granted to (say) all green-eyed males would be unfair? Why are we sure that responsibility for the critically ill and injured is relevant to the question of permitted speeds, whereas eye color and sex are not? The answer, I think, must appeal to "the object which the law in question is admittedly designed to realize."[10] The object of speed laws is to prevent automobile accidents and thus protect the health, lives, and property of motorists, passengers, and pedestrians. If we treat ambulances rushing victims to emergency medical treatment on the same footing as all other motorists bent on their private business, we will be hindering the very purpose for which we regulate automobile speeds. There is, on the other hand, no known causal connection between eye color or sex and the avowed objective of speed laws. They are, therefore, *irrelevant to that purpose,* and legal discriminations based on them are arbitrary, hence, unfair. These are judgments about relevance on which all rational men must agree. Disagreement over relevance is more likely to be intractable when the objectives of a law themselves are in dispute, especially when the given law has several purposes in uneasy tandem.

I have distinguished two ways in which the administration of law can be unjust, but there is still a third way to be mentioned. In the first example, the enforcement of a general rule is irregular, corrupt, or favoritistic. In the second instance, the statute itself is unjust because it discriminates against classes of persons who differ in respects that are not relevant to the agreed-upon objectives of the law. We have seen that an unfair law can be fairly administered and that a perfectly fair law can be unfairly administered, and that both the law and its administration can be unfair together or fair together. But now there is a third case: *the purpose of the law itself may be arbitrary and invidious.* The statute may have been consciously designed to achieve a result that is unjust, such as the conservation of economic advantage for a favored class as an end in itself (quite apart from what the "public interest" may indicate), a legal arrangement designed to ensure that one group profit at the expense of another.

The leading historical instance of the use of law for the specific purpose

---

10 Hart, *The Concept of Law,* p. 159.

of discrimination is that of Nazi Germany, 1933–1945. Imagine a Nazi law prescribing methods for the expropriation and reassignment of Jewish businesses and financial holdings. The aim of such a law, let us suppose, was to benefit "Aryans" at the expense of Jews, with no more ultimate goal in sight. That legislative purpose was to bring about a *state of affairs*, an established redistribution, that would be unjust in that it would be arbitrarily unequal in its benefits. German Jews did not differ from other Germans in any "relevant respect" justicizing this new arrangement. The motive of the legislation was *partiality*, with no cloak of fairness, and the authoritative act of legislating was therefore a plain "grab."

Now suppose that the Nazi legislature made arbitrary exceptions of red-haired Jews (perhaps because of bribery from or simple favoritism to a given red-haired Jewish millionaire with powerful connections abroad), and that this exemption was actually put into the expropriation statute. This would add to the injustice on the level of legislative purpose another injustice this time of our second type, an exemption that is plainly arbitrary because of the causal irrelevance of the class defining characteristics of the exempted class to the understood purpose of the law. But it is not clear whether the unfair exemption in the statute with the unfair objective makes the resultant law more or less unjust on the whole. Expropriated Jews could complain that their arbitrarily favored brethren are spared the hardships inflicted on them; on the other hand, they could consider that these exceptions constitute reductions in the "amount" of injustice created by the law. After all, though red-headedness is an irrelevant ground of difference among Jews, so is red-headed Jewishness an irrelevant ground of difference among the wider class of Germans. Thus, the special treatment of red-headed Jews is a comparative justice when compared to that of all non-Jewish Germans, but a comparative injustice when compared to that of all other German Jews. To ask whether the immunity for redheads is fair or unfair "on the whole" is like asking whether a woman who is tall when compared to mice, children, and other women, but short when compared to men, elephants, and office buildings, is tall or short "on the whole."

Now imagine that the Jewish expropriation bill with its exemption for redheads is passed into law. Several months later, a corrupt policeman and a corrupt judge, covering their actions with lies and forgeries, manage (for a suitable bribe) to get a brown-haired Jew exempted, while also illegally seizing a red-headed Jew's property. These acts are instances of arbitrary and invidious discrimination, through corruption, partiality, or prejudice, in the administration of general rules. How they affect the justice "on balance" of law enforcement already so unjust because of unfair exemptions in the law and an unfair legislative purpose is quite unclear. Again we shall have to define our comparison classes precisely, and make conflicting relational judgments. It is unfair to the other brown-haired Jews to let this one off when they are all forced into poverty and misery (though it is doubtful that people already so persecuted will feel still more aggrieved; they may even *rejoice* at their comrade's good luck); it also seems unfair to the framed red-headed Jew when his treatment is compared to that of *other* red-headed Jews. On the other hand, there is no injustice in the exoneration of the brown-headed Jew when his treatment is compared to that of non-Jewish businessmen, nor is the framed red-headed Jew treated unfairly in comparison to all brown-headed Jews. Balancing these judgments is complicated further by the problem of deciding whether characteristics that are "relevant" *only* because an unfair law says they are (red-headedness, Jewishness) should be given any weight at all.

But we shall go no farther with the problem here. These examples are designed only to show that occasions for justice involving general rules are of three kinds—at the levels of administration, legislative formulation, and legislative purpose; that injustice is possible at all three levels; and that injustice at one level affects the moral quality of acts at the other levels in unclear ways, capable of being spelled out only in limited comparative judgments. Just as the irrelevance of a "respect" used as a ground of discrimination at level two cannot be shown by the law itself but only by reference to the law's purpose, so also the irrelevance of a respect used to ground discrimination at level three cannot be shown by the legislative purpose itself, but only by reference to other extralegal standards. The way to test the relevance of discriminatory grounds in the legislative purpose is to examine the *state of affairs* to be produced by the law to see whether it includes deprivations, inequalities, and disadvantages suffered by some classes without good reason. The question of what constitutes a good reason at this level brings us to our next problem.

5. ECONOMIC INCOME

The term "distributive justice" traditionally applied to burdens and benefits directly distributed by political authorities, such as appointed offices, welfare doles, taxes, and military conscription, but it has now come to apply also to goods and evils of a nonpolitical kind that can be distributed by private citizens to other private citizens. In fact, in most recent literature, the term is reserved for *economic* distributions, particularly the justice of differences in economic income between classes, and of various schemes of taxation which discriminate in different ways between classes. Further, the phrase can refer not only to acts of distributing but also to de facto states of affairs, such as *the fact that* at present "the five percent at the top get 20 percent [of our national wealth] while the 20 percent at the bottom get about five percent."[11] There is, of course, an ambiguity in the meaning of "distribu-

---

11 "T.R.B. from Washington" in *The New Republic,* Vol. CLX, No. 12 (March 22, 1969), p. 4.

tion." The word may refer to the *process* of distributing, or the *product* of some process of distributing, and either or both of these can be appraised as just or unjust. In addition, a "distribution" can be understood to be a "product" which is *not* the result of any deliberate distributing process, but simply a state of affairs whose production has been too complicated to summarize or to ascribe to any definite group of persons as their deliberate doing. The present "distribution" of American wealth is just such a state of affairs.

Are the 5 percent of Americans "at the top" really different from the 20 percent "at the bottom" in any respect that would justicize the difference between their incomes? It is doubtful that there is any characteristic—relevant or irrelevant—common and peculiar to all members of either group. *Some* injustices, therefore, must surely exist. Perhaps there are some traits, however, that are more or less characteristic of the members of the privileged group, that make the current arrangements at least approximately just. What could (or should) those traits be? The answer will state a standard of relevance and a principle of material justice for questions of economic distributions, at least in relatively affluent societies like that of the United States.

At this point there appears to be no appeal possible except to *basic attitudes,* but even at this level we should avoid premature pessimism about the possibility of rational agreement. Some answers to our question have been generally discredited, and if we can see why those answers are inadequate, we might discover some important clues to the properties any adequate answer must possess. Even philosophical adversaries with strongly opposed initial attitudes may hope to come to eventual agreement if they share *some* relevant beliefs and standards and a common commitment to consistency. Let us consider why we all agree (that is the author's assumption) in rejecting the view that differences in race, sex, IQ, or social "rank" are the grounds of just differences in wealth or income. Part of the answer seems obvious. People cannot by their own voluntary choices determine what skin color, sex, or IQ they shall have, or which hereditary caste they shall enter. To make such properties the basis of discrimination between individuals in the distribution of social benefits would be "to treat people differently in ways that profoundly affect their lives because of differences for which they have no responsibility."[12] Differences in a given respect are *relevant* for the aims of distributive justice, then, only if they are differences for which their possessors can be held responsible; properties can be the grounds of just discrimination between persons only if those persons had a *fair opportunity* to acquire or avoid them. Having rejected a number of material principles that clearly fail to satisfy the "fair opportunity" require-

[12] W. K. Frankena, "Some Beliefs About Justice," *The Lindley Lecture,* Department of Philosophy Pamphlet (Lawrence: University of Kansas, 1966), p. 10.

ment, we are still left with as many as five candidates for our acceptance.
(It is in theory open to us to accept two or more of these five as valid
principles, there being no a priori necessity that the list be reduced to one.)
These are: (1) the principle of perfect equality; (2) the principle[s] of
need; (3) the principles of merit and achievement; (4) the principle of
contribution (or due return); (5) the principle of effort (or labor). I shall
discuss each of these briefly.

(i) EQUALITY

The principle of perfect equality obviously has a place in any adequate
social ethic. Every human being is equally a human being, and as we saw in
Chapter 6, that minimal qualification entitles all human beings equally to
certain absolute human rights: positive rights to noneconomic "goods" that
by their very natures cannot be in short supply, negative rights not to be
treated in cruel or inhuman ways, and negative rights not to be exploited
or degraded even in "humane" ways. It is quite another thing, however, to
make the minimal qualification of humanity the ground for an absolutely
equal distribution of a country's *material wealth* among its citizens. A strict
equalitarian could argue that he is merely applying Aristotle's formula of
proportionate equality (presumably accepted by all parties to the dispute)
with a criterion of relevance borrowed from the human rights theorists.
Thus, distributive justice is accomplished between A and B when the following ratio is satisfied:

$$\frac{A\text{'s share of } P}{B\text{'s share of } P} = \frac{A\text{'s possession of } Q}{B\text{'s possession of } Q}$$

Where P stands for economic goods, Q must stand simply for "humanity"
or "a human nature," and since every human being possesses *that* Q equally,
it follows that all should also share a society's economic wealth (the P in
question) equally.

The trouble with this argument is that its major premise is no less
disputable than its conclusion. The standard of relevance it borrows from
other contexts where it seems very little short of self-evident, seems controversial, at best, when applied to purely economic contexts. It seems
evident to most of us that merely being human entitles *everyone*—bad men
as well as good, lazy as well as industrious, inept as well as skilled—to a
fair trial if charged with a crime, to equal protection of the law, to equal
consideration of his interests by makers of national policy, to be spared
torture or other cruel and inhuman treatment, and to be permanently
ineligible for the status of chattel slave. Adding a right to an equal share
of the economic pie, however, is to add a benefit of a wholly different order,
one whose presence on the list of goods for which mere humanity is the
sole qualifying condition is not likely to win wide assent without further
argument.

It is far more plausible to posit a human right to the satisfaction of (better: to an opportunity to satisfy) one's *basic* economic needs, that is, to enough food and medicine to remain healthy, to minimal clothing, housing, and so on. As Hume pointed out,[13] even these rights cannot exist under conditions of extreme scarcity. Where there is not enough to go around, it cannot be true that everyone has a right to an equal share.[14] But wherever there is moderate abundance or better—wherever a society produces more than enough to satisfy the *basic needs of everyone*—there it seems more plausible to say that mere possession of basic human needs qualifies a person for the opportunity to satisfy them. It would be a rare and calloused sense of justice that would not be offended by an affluent society, with a large annual agricultural surplus and a great abundance of manufactured goods, which permitted some of its citizens to die of starvation, exposure, or easily curable disease. It would certainly be *unfair* for a nation to produce more than it needs and not permit some of its citizens enough to satisfy their basic biological requirements. Strict equalitarianism, then, is a perfectly plausible material principle of distributive justice when confined to affluent societies and basic biological needs, but it loses plausibility when applied to division of the "surplus" left over after basic needs are met. To be sure, the greater the degree of affluence, the higher the level at which we might draw the line between "basic needs" and merely "wanted" benefits, and insofar as social institutions create "artificial needs," it is only fair that society provide all with the opportunity to satisfy them.[15] But once the line has been drawn between what is needed to live a minimally decent life by the realistic standards of a given time and place and what is only added "gravy," it is far from evident that justice still insists upon absolutely equal shares of the total. And it is evident that justice does *not* require strict equality wherever there is reason to think that unequal distribution causally determines greater production and is in the interests of everyone, even those who receive the relatively smaller shares.

Still, there is no way to *refute* the strict equalitarian who requires exactly equal shares for everyone whenever that can be arranged without discouraging total productivity to the point where everyone loses. No one would insist upon equal distributions that would diminish the size of the total pie and leave smaller slices for *everyone;* that would be opposed to reason. John Rawls makes this condition part of his "rational principle" of justice: "Inequalities are arbitrary unless it is reasonable to expect that

[13] David Hume, *Enquiry Concerning the Principles of Morals* Part III (LaSalle, Ill.: The Open Court Publishing Company, 1947). Originally published in 1777.

[14] Except in the "manifesto sense" of "right" discussed on p. 67.

[15] This point is well made by Katzner, "An Analysis of the Concept of Justice," pp. 173–203.

they will work out to everyone's advantage. . . ."[16] We are left then with a
version of strict equalitarianism that is by no means evidently true and yet
is impossible to refute. That is the theory that purports to apply not only to
basic needs but to the total wealth of a society, and allows departures from
strict equality when, *but only when*, they will work out to everyone's
advantage. Although I am not persuaded by this theory, I think that any
adequate material principle will have to attach great importance to keeping
differences in wealth within reasonable limits, even after all basic needs
have been met. One way of doing this would be to raise the standards for
a "basic need" as total wealth goes up, so that differences between the richest
and poorest citizens (even when there is no real "poverty") are kept within
moderate limits.

(ii) NEED

The principle of need is subject to various interpretations, but in most
of its forms it is not an independent principle at all, but only a way of
mediating the application of the principle of equality. It can, therefore, be
grouped with the principle of perfect equality as a member of the equalitarian family and contrasted with the principles of merit, achievement, contribution, and effort, which are all members of the nonequalitarian family.
Consider some differences in "needs" as they bear on distributions. Doe is
a bachelor with no dependents; Roe has a wife and six children. Roe must
satisfy the needs of eight persons out of his paycheck, whereas Doe need
satisfy the needs of only one. To give Roe and Doe equal pay would be
to treat Doe's interests substantially *more* generously than those of anyone
in the Roe family. Similarly, if a small private group is distributing food to
its members (say a shipwrecked crew waiting rescue on a desert island), it
would not be fair to give precisely the same quantity to a one hundred
pounder as to a two hundred pounder, for that might be giving one person
all he needs and the other only a fraction of what he needs—a difference
in treatment not supported by any relevant difference between them. In
short, to distribute goods in proportion to basic needs is not really to depart
from a standard of equality, but rather to bring those with some greater
initial burden or deficit up to the same level as their fellows.

The concept of a "need" is extremely elastic. In a general sense, to say
that S needs X is to say simply that if he doesn't have X he will be harmed.
A "basic need" would then be for an X in whose absence a person would be
harmed in some crucial and fundamental way, such as suffering injury,
malnutrition, illness, madness, or premature death. Thus we all have a basic
need for foodstuffs of a certain quantity and variety, fuel to heat our
dwellings, a roof over our heads, clothing to keep us warm, and so on. In

16 John Rawls, "Justice as Fairness," *The Philosophical Review*, LXVII (1958), 165.

a different but related sense of need, to say that S needs X is to say that without X he cannot achieve some specific purpose or perform some specific function. If they are to do their work, carpenters need tools, merchants need capital and customers, authors need paper and publishers. Some helpful goods are not strictly needed in this sense: an author with pencil and paper does not really need a typewriter to write a book, but he may need it to write a book speedily, efficiently, and conveniently. We sometimes come to rely upon "merely helpful but unneeded goods" to such a degree that we develop a strong habitual dependence on them, in which case (as it is often said) we have a "psychological" as opposed to a material need for them. If we don't possess that for which we have a strong psychological need, we may be unable to be happy, in which case a merely psychological need for a functional instrument may become a genuine need in the first sense distinguished above, namely, something whose absence is harmful to us. (Cutting across the distinction between material and psychological needs is that between "natural" and "artificial" needs, the former being those that can be expected to develop in any normal person, the latter being those that are manufactured or contrived, and somehow implanted in, or imposed upon, a person.) The more abundant a society's material goods, the higher the level at which we are required (by the force of psychological needs) to fix the distinction between "necessities" and "luxuries"; what *everyone* in a given society regards as "necessary" tends to become an actual, basic need.

(iii) MERIT AND ACHIEVEMENT

The remaining three candidates for material principles of distributive justice belong to the nonequalitarian family. These three principles would each distribute goods in accordance, not with need, but with *desert;* since persons obviously differ in their deserts, economic goods would be distributed unequally. The three principles differ from one another in their conceptions of the relevant *bases of desert* for economic distributions. The first is the principle of *merit.* Unlike the other principles in the nonequalitarian family, this one focuses not on what a person has *done* to deserve his allotment, but rather on what kind of person he is—what characteristics he has.

Two different types of characteristic might be considered meritorious in the appropriate sense: skills and virtues. Native skills and inherited aptitudes will not be appropriate desert bases, since they are forms of merit ruled out by the fair opportunity requirement. No one deserves credit or blame for his genetic inheritance, since no one has the opportunity to select his own genes. Acquired skills may seem more plausible candidates at first, but upon scrutiny they are little better. First, all acquired skills depend to a large degree on native skills. Nobody is born knowing how to read, so reading is an acquired skill, but actual differences in reading skill are to a large degree accounted for by genetic differences that are beyond anyone's control. Some of the differences are no doubt caused by differences in motivation afforded different children, but again the early conditions contributing to a child's motivation are also largely beyond his control. We may still have some differences in acquired skills that are to be accounted for solely or primarily by differences in the degree of practice, drill, and perseverance expended by persons with roughly equal opportunities. In respect to these, we can propitiate the requirement of fair opportunity, but only by nullifying the significance of acquired skill as such, for now skill is a relevant basis of desert only to the extent that it is a product of one's own effort. Hence, *effort* becomes the true basis of desert (as claimed by our fifth principle, discussed below), and not simply skill as such.

Those who would propose rewarding personal *virtues* with a larger than average share of the economic pie, and punishing defects of character with a smaller than average share, advocate assigning to the economic system a task normally done (if it is done at all) by noneconomic institutions. What they propose, in effect, is that we use retributive criteria of distributive justice. Our criminal law, for a variety of good reasons, does not purport to punish people for what they are, but only for what they do. A man can be as arrogant, rude, selfish, cruel, insensitive, irresponsible, cowardly, lazy, or disloyal as he wishes; unless he *does* something prohibited by the criminal law, he will not be made to suffer legal punishment. At least one of the legal system's reasons for refusing to penalize character flaws as such would also explain why such defects should not be listed as relevant differences in a material principle of distributive justice. The apparatus for detecting such flaws (a "moral police"?) would be enormously cumbersome and impractical, and its methods so uncertain and fallible that none of us could feel safe in entrusting the determination of our material allotments to it. We could, of course, give roughly equal shares to all except those few who have *outstanding* virtues—gentleness, kindness, courage, diligence, reliability, warmth, charm, considerateness, generosity. Perhaps these are traits that deserve to be rewarded, but it is doubtful that larger economic allotments are the appropriate vehicles of rewarding. As Benn and Peters remind us, "there are some sorts of 'worth' for which rewards in terms of income seem inappropriate. Great courage in battle is recognized by medals, not by increased pay."[17] Indeed, there is something repugnant, as Socrates and the Stoics insisted, in paying a man to be virtuous. Moreover, the rewards would offer a pecuniary motive for certain forms of excellence that require motives of a different kind, and would thus tend to be self-defeating.

The most plausible nonequalitarian theories are those that locate relevance not in meritorious traits and excellences of any kind, but rather in prior doings: not in what one is, but in what one has done. Actions, too, are

---

17 Benn and Peters, *Social Principles and the Democratic State*, p. 139.

sometimes called "meritorious," so there is no impropriety in denominating the remaining families of principles in our survey as "meritarian." One type of action-oriented meritarian might cite *achievement* as a relevant desert basis for pecuniary rewards, so that departures from equality in income are to be justicized only by distinguished achievements in science, art, philosophy, music, athletics, and other basic areas of human activity. The attractions and disadvantages of this theory are similar to those of theories which I rejected above that base rewards on skills and virtues. Not all persons have a fair opportunity to achieve great things, and economic rewards seem inappropriate as vehicles for expressing recognition and admiration of noneconomic achievements.

(iv) CONTRIBUTION OR "DUE RETURN"

When the achievements under consideration are themselves contributions to our general economic well-being, the meritarian principle of distributive justice is much more plausible. Often it is conjoined with an economic theory that purports to determine exactly what percentage of our total economic product a given worker or class has produced. Justice, according to this principle, requires that each worker get back exactly that proportion of the national wealth that he has himself created. This sounds very much like a principle of "commutative justice" directing us to *give back* to every worker what is really his own property, that is, the product of his own labor.

The French socialist writer and precursor of Karl Marx, Pierre Joseph Proudhon (1809–1865), is perhaps the classic example of this kind of theorist. In his book, *What Is Property?* (1840), Proudhon rejects the standard socialist slogan, "From each according to his ability, to each according to his needs,"[18] in favor of a principle of distributive justice based on contribution, as interpreted by an economic theory that employed a pre-Marxist "theory of surplus value." The famous socialist slogan was not intended, in any case, to express a principle of distributive justice. It was understood to be a rejection of all considerations of "mere" justice for an ethic of human brotherhood. The early socialists thought it unfair, in a way, to give the great contributors to our wealth a disproportionately small share of the product. But in the new socialist society, love of neighbor, community spirit, and absence of avarice would overwhelm such bourgeois notions and put them in their proper (subordinate) place.

Proudhon, on the other hand, based his whole social philosophy not on brotherhood (an ideal he found suitable only for small groups such as

---

18 Traced to Louis Blanc. For a clear brief exposition of Proudhon's view which contrasts it with that of other early socialists and also that of Karl Marx, see Robert Tucker's "Marx and Distributive Justice," in *Nomos VI: Justice,* ed. C. J. Friedrich and J. W. Chapman (New York: Aldine-Atherton Press, 1963), pp. 306–25.

families) but on the kind of distributive justice to which even some
capitalists gave lip service:

The key concept was "mutuality" or "reciprocity." "Mutuality, reciprocity exists,"
he wrote, "when all the workers in an industry, instead of working for an entre-
preneur who pays them and keeps their products, work for one another and thus
collaborate in the making of a common product whose profits they share among
themselves."[19]

Proudhon's celebrated dictum that "property is theft" did not imply that
all *possession* of goods is illicit, but rather that the system of rules that
permitted the owner of a factory to hire workers and draw profits ("surplus
value") from *their* labor robs the workers of what is rightly theirs. "This
profit, consisting of a portion of the proceeds of labor that rightfully
belonged to the laborer himself, was 'theft.' "[20] The injustice of capitalism,
according to Proudhon, consists in the fact that those who create the wealth
(through their labor) get only a small part of what they create, whereas
those who "exploit" their labor, like voracious parasites, gather in a greatly
disproportionate share. The "return of contribution" principle of distributive justice, then, cannot work in a capitalist system, but requires a *fédération
mutualiste* of autonomous producer-cooperatives in which those who create
wealth by their work share it in proportion to their real contributions.

Other theorists, employing different notions of what produces or "creates"
economic wealth, have used the "return of contribution" principle to support
quite opposite conclusions. The contribution principle has even been used to
justicize quite unequalitarian capitalistic status quos, for it is said that capital
as well as labor creates wealth, as do ingenious ideas, inventions, and
adventurous risk-taking. The capitalist who provided the money, the inventor
who designed a product to be manufactured, the innovator who thought
of a new mode of production and marketing, the advertiser who persuaded
millions of customers to buy the finished product, the investor who risked
his savings on the success of the enterprise—these are the ones, it is said,
who did the most to produce the wealth created by a business, not the
workers who contributed only their labor, and of course, these are the ones
who tend, on the whole, to receive the largest personal incomes.

Without begging any narrow and technical questions of economics, I
should express my general skepticism concerning such facile generalizations
about the comparative degrees to which various individuals have contributed
to our social wealth. Not only are there impossibly difficult problems of
measurement involved, there are also conceptual problems that appear
beyond all nonarbitrary solution. I refer to the elements of luck and chance,
the social factors not attributable to any assignable individuals, and the

19 Tucker, "Marx and Distributive Justice," p. 310.
20 Tucker, "Marx and Distributive Justice," p. 311.

contributions of population trends, uncreated natural resources, and the efforts of people now dead, which are often central to the explanation of any given increment of social wealth.

The difficulties of separating out causal factors in the production of social wealth might influence the partisan of the "return of contribution" principle in either or both of two ways. He might become very cautious in his application of the principle, requiring that deviations from average shares be restricted to very clear and demonstrable instances of unusually great or small contributions. But the moral that L. T. Hobhouse[21] drew from these difficulties is that *any* individual contribution will be very small relative to the immeasurably great contribution made by political, social, fortuitous, natural, and "inherited" factors. In particular, strict application of the "return of contribution" principle would tend to support a larger claim for the *community* to its own "due return," through taxation and other devices.

In a way, the principle of contribution is not a principle of mere *desert* at all, no matter how applied. As mentioned above, it resembles a principle of commutative justice requiring repayment of debts, return of borrowed items, or compensation for wrongly inflicted damages. If I lend you my car on the understanding that you will take good care of it and soon return it, or if you steal it, or damage it, it will be too *weak* to say that I "deserve" to have my own car, intact, back from you. After all, the car is *mine* or my due, and questions of ownership are not settled by examination of deserts; neither are considerations of ownership and obligation commonly outbalanced by considerations of desert. It is not merely "unfitting" or "inappropriate" that I should not have my own or my due; it is downright *theft* to withhold it from me. So the return of contribution is not merely a matter of merit deserving reward. It is a matter of a maker demanding that which he has created and is thus properly his. The ratio—A's share of X is to B's share of X as A's contribution to X is to B's contribution to X—appears, therefore, to be a very strong and plausible principle of distributive justice, whose main deficiencies, when applied to economic distributions, are of a practical (though severe) kind. If Hobhouse is right in claiming that there are social factors in even the most pronounced individual contributions to social wealth, then the principle of due return serves as a moral basis in support of taxation and other public claims to private goods. In any case, if A's contribution, though apparently much greater than B's, is nevertheless only the tiniest percentage of the total contribution to X (whatever that may mean and however it is to be determined), it may seem like the meanest quibbling to distinguish very seriously between A and B at all.

[21] L. T. Hobhouse, *The Elements of Social Justice* (London: George Allen and Unwin Ltd., 1922). See especially pp. 161–63.

(v) EFFORT

The principle of due return, as a material principle of distributive justice, does have some vulnerability to the fair opportunity requirement. Given unavoidable variations in genetic endowments and material circumstances, different persons cannot have precisely the same opportunities to make contributions to the public weal. Our final candidate for the status of a material principle of distributive justice, the *principle of effort,* does much better in this respect, for it would distribute economic products not in proportion to successful achievement but according to the degree of effort exerted. According to the principle of effort, justice decrees that hardworking executives and hard-working laborers receive precisely the same remuneration (although there may be reasons having nothing to do with justice for paying more to the executives), and that freeloaders be penalized by allotments of proportionately lesser shares of the joint products of everyone's labor. The most persuasive argument for this principle is that it is the closest approximation to the intuitively valid principle of due return that can pass the fair opportunity requirement. It is doubtful, however, that even the principle of effort fully satisfies the requirement of fair opportunity, since those who inherit or acquire certain kinds of handicap may have little opportunity to *acquire the motivation* even to do their best. In any event, the principle of effort does seem to have intuitive cogency giving it at least some weight as a factor determining the justice of distributions.

In very tentative conclusion, it seems that the principle of equality (in the version that rests on needs rather than that which requires "perfect equality") and the principles of contribution and effort (where nonarbitrarily applicable, and only *after* everyone's basic needs have been satisfied) have the most weight as determinants of economic justice, whereas all forms of the principle of merit are implausible in that role. The reason for the priority of basic needs is that, where there is economic abundance, the claim to life itself and to minimally decent conditions are, like other human rights, claims that all men make with perfect equality. As economic production increases, these claims are given ever greater consideration in the form of rising standards for distinguishing basic needs from other wanted goods. But no matter where that line is drawn, when we go beyond it into the realm of economic surplus or "luxuries," nonequalitarian considerations (especially contribution and effort) come increasingly into play.

6. FAIR PROCEDURES AND JUST OUTCOMES We have been concerned here only with the character of just results considered in total abstraction from the procedures that can be used to bring them about. Indeed, we have considered characterizations of just results for use as *tests* of the fairness of procedures, on the assumption that the only standard for the fairness or unfairness of a procedure is the degree to which it conduces to just results. But is it really possible to treat the questions of fair procedures and just results in such strict isolation from one another?

John Rawls has made some useful distinctions that will facilitate our discussion of the relation between distributive economic institutions and practices and resultant patterns of wealth distribution. In a recent book,[22] Rawls distinguishes among three types of "procedural justice" in terms of their relations to the justice of outcomes. *Perfect procedural justice* is illustrated by the stock example of men dividing a cake. The procedure adopted to bring about the correct result (here assumed to be equal shares) is for the man who cuts the slices to be the last to choose his own portion. Only if he cuts the cake into equal slices is he sure of getting the largest share possible under the adopted procedural rule. This situation exemplifies perfect procedural justice because it satisfies the following two conditions: (1) there is an independent criterion for what is a just result (fair division), defined separately from and prior to the selection of a procedure to be followed, and (2) it is possible to design a procedure (e.g., the cake-cutter chooses last) that is likely to give the proper result. *Imperfect procedural justice* is illustrated by a criminal trial. It is like perfect procedural justice in that there is an independent criterion for the right result; but unlike it in that there is *no* feasible procedure certain to lead to just results in every case. The fairness of the procedural rules is determined entirely by their conducibility *in general* to just results, but there is no guarantee that even the most fastidious adherence to the rules will lead to a just outcome in a given case.

What Rawls calls *pure procedural justice* differs from both perfect and imperfect procedural justice in that there is *no* independent criterion for the just result. "Instead, there is a correct or fair procedure such that the outcome is likewise correct or fair, whatever it is, provided that the procedure has been properly followed."[23] Betting and certain other forms of gambling illustrate this third type of procedural justice. The redistribution of funds among a group of gamblers, as a result of their wagers or games, is fair, *whatever it is,* if and only if antecedently defined betting procedures have been scrupulously adhered to, with no cheating and no coercion.

If we assume that the criterion of a just outcome for distributions of economic goods *can* be defined independently of the rules of any given procedure for distributing those goods, and can be used therefore as a test of the fairness of alternative procedures, then we must take the context of economic distribution to exemplify what Rawls calls "imperfect procedural justice." When we choose from the point of view of fairness among various

[22] John Rawls, *A Theory of Justice* (Cambridge: Harvard University Press, 1971), pp. 84–86.

[23] Rawls, *A Theory of Justice,* p. 86.

capitalist, socialist, and mixed schemes for organizing an economy, we cannot hope to find a system that is certain to generate a just outcome in every instance, giving every citizen exactly his due as determined by an independent material criterion of distributive justice. Even assuming agreement on the criterion of a just distributive outcome, our choice is more like that between rival procedures for conducting a criminal trial, e.g., between the adversary system used in English-speaking countries and the inquisitorial system used elsewhere in Europe. For criminal trials we have an agreed upon conception of just outcomes: we want guilty men convicted and innocent men acquitted. What we must decide is, which alternative system of criminal procedure, subject to certain obvious restrictions set by other values, is likely to achieve these objectives in the higher percentage of cases? Similarly, in the choice among economic systems on the assumption of independent standards for just outcomes, we must decide which of the alternative systems of procedures will come closest to satisfying those standards, subject to the restrictions of such other values as efficiency and liberty.

On the other hand, we might prefer to take the problem of economic distribution to be a question of what Rawls calls "pure procedural justice," at least for that part of the problem that concerns the economic "surplus" that is left after basic needs have been satisfied equally for everyone. Our choice will hinge in large part on whether we take the economic arena to be basically cooperative or competitive, whether we think of our economic interrelations as a race for surplus riches with economic income as prizes for the swiftest, or "winnings" for the luckiest, or as some other kind of rule-governed "game" we all play or contest we all enter. In the end, our criteria of economic justice will reflect the way we *conceive* the economic sphere of life. Beyond the level of basic needs (interpreted in a realistic and generous way), even the model of the roulette wheel with its simple rules of pure procedural justice provides a possible, if unappealing, model. Given the universal satisfaction of basic human needs, those procedures for producing and distributing goods are best that best promote the common good, and there may be no clear and convincing criterion for the just distribution of "surplus goods" other than the fair operation of those procedures, whichever they may be.

FOR FURTHER READING

CHAPTER 1. THE CONCEPT OF FREEDOM

BENN, S. I., and W. WEINSTEIN, "Being Free to Act, and Being a Free Man," *Mind*, LXXX (1971), pp. 194–211.

BERLIN, ISAIAH, *Four Essays on Liberty*. London, Oxford: Oxford University Press, 1969.

CRANSTON, MAURICE, *Freedom, A New Analysis*. London: Longmans, Green & Co. Ltd., 1953.

LEWIS, C. S., *Studies in Words*. Cambridge: Cambridge University Press, 1961, Chap. 5 ("Free").

MACCALLUM, GERALD C., JR., "Negative and Positive Freedom," *Philosophical Review*, LXXVI (1967), 312–334.

OPPENHEIM, FELIX, *Dimensions of Freedom*. New York: St. Martin's Press, Inc., 1961.

CHAPTER 2. GROUNDS FOR COERCION

HART, H. L. A., *Law, Liberty, and Morality*. Stanford, Calif.: Stanford University Press, 1963.

HOBHOUSE, L. T., *Elements of Social Justice*. London: George Allen and Unwin Ltd., 1922, Chap. 4.

———, *Liberalism*. New York: Holt, Rinehart and Winston, Inc., 1911.

MILL, J. S., *On Liberty*. New York: Liberal Arts Press, 1956.

STEPHEN, J. F., *Liberty, Equality, and Fraternity*. Cambridge: Cambridge University Press, 1967.

CHAPTER 3. HARD CASES FOR THE HARM PRINCIPLE

CARE, NORMAN, and THOMAS TRELOGAN, eds., *Issues in Law and Morality*. Cleveland: Case Western Reserve Press, 1973.

OLSON, MANCUR, *The Logic of Collective Action*. Cambridge, Mass.: Harvard University Press, 1965.

WASSERSTROM, R., ed., *Morality and the Law*. Belmont, Calif.: Wadsworth Publishing Co., 1971.

CHAPTER 4. LEGAL RIGHTS

BENN, S. I., and R. S. PETERS, *Social Principles and the Democratic State.* London: George Allen and Unwin Ltd., 1959, pp. 88–95.

SALMOND, JOHN, *Jurisprudence* (11th ed.), ed. by Glanville Williams. London: Sweet & Maxwell, Ltd., 1967, Chaps. 10, 11.

WASSERSTROM, R., "Rights, Human Rights, and Racial Discrimination," *Journal of Philosophy,* LXI (1964), 628–41.

CHAPTER 5. CONFLICTS OF LEGAL RIGHTS

FRANTZ, LAURENT B., "The First Amendment in the Balance," *Yale Law Journal,* LXXI (1962), pp. 1424–50.

GIANNELLA, DONALD, "The Religious Liberty Guarantee," *Harvard Law Review,* LXXX (1967), pp. 1381–1431.

CHAPTER 6. HUMAN RIGHTS

MELDEN, A. I., *Rights and Right Conduct.* Oxford: Basil Blackwell, 1959, esp. Parts 3–6.

The Monist, Issue on "Human Rights," LII (1968).

VLASTOS, GREGORY, "Justice and Equality," in *Social Justice,* ed. by Richard B. Brandt. Englewood Cliffs, N.J.: Prentice-Hall, Inc., 1962, pp. 31–72.

WILLIAMS, B. A. O., "The Idea of Equality," in *Philosophy, Politics, and Society,* ed. by P. Laslett and W. G. Runciman. New York: Barnes & Noble, Inc., 1962, pp. 110–31.

CHAPTER 7. SOCIAL JUSTICE

FRANKENA, W. K., "Some Beliefs About Justice," *The Lindley Lecture,* Department of Philosophy Pamphlet. Lawrence: University of Kansas, 1966.

FRIEDRICH, C. J., and J. CHAPMAN, eds., *Nomos VI: Justice.* New York: Aldine-Atherton, 1963.

HOBHOUSE, L. T., *Elements of Social Justice.* London: George Allen and Unwin Ltd., 1922, Chap. 9 ("Social and Personal Factors in Wealth").

KATZNER, LOUIS, "Presumptivist and Nonpresumptivist Principles of Formal Justice," *Ethics,* LXXXI (1971), pp. 253–58.

RAWLS, JOHN, *A Theory of Justice.* Cambridge, Mass.: Harvard University Press, 1971.

RESCHER, NICHOLAS, *Distributive Justice.* Indianapolis: The Bobbs-Merrill Co., Inc., 1966.

INDEX

Acton, H. B., 64
American Civil Liberties Union, 42–43
Ames, James Barr, 29n.
Anarchistic principle, 22–24
Animals:
  cruelty to, 36, 41, 86, 98n.
  rights of, 85, 86, 96
Anomie, 14
Aristotle, 100, 109
Autonomy, 14–17

Bad examples, 32
Barenblatt v. United States, 79
Bayles, Michael, 34
Benn, S.I., and Peters, R.S., 61n., 72n.,
  100n., 113, 121
Benn, S.I., and Wienstein, W., 120
Bentham, Jeremy, 23
Berlin, Sir Isaiah, 8n., 9, 16n., 99n., 120
Black, Justice Hugo, 79
Blanc, Louis, 114n.
Brandt, Richard B., 74
Brave New World, 9
Broad, C.D., 40n.

Care, Norman, 120
Chapman, J. (*see* Friedrich, C.J., and
  Chapman, J.)
Civil disobedience, 38–39
Claim, concept of, 2, 64–67
Claim-rights:
  classification, 59–61
  definition, 58
  value, 58–59
Clear and present danger, 42
Coercion, 7, 11, 20–35
Coherence, 3
Collective goods, 53–54

*Communist Party v. Subversive Activities
  Control Board,* 80
Compulsion (*see* Constraint)
Conceptual problems, 1
Consent, 46
Conservatives, 11
Constraint:
  absence of, and self-government, 16–17
  as opposed to compulsion, 5n.
  as opposed to inability, 8–9
  external, 12–13
  internal, 9, 12–13
  negative, 9, 12–13
  positive, 12–13
Contentment (*see* Want satisfaction)
Contribution, as principle of distributive
  justice, 114–16
Corbin, Arthur L., 56n., 58
Corpses, mistreatment of, 36–37
Correlativity of rights and duties:
  logical, 62–64
  moral, 61–63
Cranston, Maurice, 5n., 11, 120

Dennis v. United States, 80
Desert, 112, 116
Devlin, Patrick, 37–39
Drugs, harmful, 50–52, 92, 96
Drunkenness, 31–32, 48, 49
Due return (*see* Contribution)
Durkheim, Emile, 14
Duty, concept of, 63

Economic freedom (*see* Freedom)
Economic justice (*see* Justice)
Effort, as principle of distributive justice,
  117
Elliptical expressions, 5, 11

123